Amazon CloudWatch Events User Guide

A catalogue record for this book is available from the Hong Kong Public Libraries.

Published in Hong Kong by Samurai Media Limited.

Email: info@samuraimedia.org

ISBN 9789888408146

Contents

What is Amazon CloudWatch Events?

Amazon CloudWatch Events delivers a near real-time stream of system events that describe changes in Amazon Web Services (AWS) resources. Using simple rules that you can quickly set up, you can match events and route them to one or more target functions or streams. CloudWatch Events becomes aware of operational changes as they occur. CloudWatch Events responds to these operational changes and takes corrective action as necessary, by sending messages to respond to the environment, activating functions, making changes, and capturing state information.

You can also use CloudWatch Events to schedule automated actions that self-trigger at certain times using cron or rate expressions. For more information, see Schedule Expressions for Rules.

You can configure the following AWS services as targets for CloudWatch Events:

- Amazon EC2 instances
- AWS Lambda functions
- Streams in Amazon Kinesis Data Streams
- Delivery streams in Amazon Kinesis Data Firehose
- Amazon ECS tasks
- SSM Run Command
- SSM Automation
- AWS Batch jobs
- Step Functions state machines
- Pipelines in AWS CodePipeline
- AWS CodeBuild projects
- Amazon Inspector assessment templates
- Amazon SNS topics
- Amazon SQS queues
- Built-in targets
- The default event bus of another AWS account

Concepts

Before you begin using CloudWatch Events, you should understand the following concepts:

- **Events**—An event indicates a change in your AWS environment. AWS resources can generate events when their state changes. For example, Amazon EC2 generates an event when the state of an EC2 instance changes from pending to running, and Amazon EC2 Auto Scaling generates events when it launches or terminates instances. AWS CloudTrail publishes events when you make API calls. You can generate custom application-level events and publish them to CloudWatch Events. You can also set up scheduled events that are generated on a periodic basis. For a list of services that generate events, and sample events from each service, see CloudWatch Events Event Examples From Each Supported Service.
- **Targets**—A target processes events. Targets can include Amazon EC2 instances, AWS Lambda functions, Kinesis streams, Amazon ECS tasks, Step Functions state machines, Amazon SNS topics, Amazon SQS queues, and built-in targets. A target receives events in JSON format.
- **Rules**—A rule matches incoming events and routes them to targets for processing. A single rule can route to multiple targets, all of which are processed in parallel. Rules are not processed in a particular order. This enables different parts of an organization to look for and process the events that are of interest to them. A rule can customize the JSON sent to the target, by passing only certain parts or by overwriting it with a constant.

Related AWS Services

The following services are used in conjunction with CloudWatch Events:

- **AWS CloudTrail** enables you to monitor the calls made to the CloudWatch Events API for your account, including calls made by the AWS Management Console, the AWS CLI and other services. When CloudTrail logging is turned on, CloudWatch Events writes log files to an S3 bucket. Each log file contains one or more records, depending on how many actions are performed to satisfy a request. For more information, see Logging Amazon CloudWatch Events API Calls in AWS CloudTrail.

- **AWS CloudFormation** enables you to model and set up your AWS resources. You create a template that describes the AWS resources you want, and AWS CloudFormation takes care of provisioning and configuring those resources for you. You can use CloudWatch Events rules in your AWS CloudFormation templates. For more information, see AWS::Events::Rule in the AWS CloudFormation User Guide.

- **AWS Config** enables you to record configuration changes to your AWS resources. This includes how resources relate to one another and how they were configured in the past, so that you can see how the configurations and relationships change over time. You can also create AWS Config rules to check whether your resources are compliant or noncompliant with your organization's policies. For more information, see the AWS Config Developer Guide.

- **AWS Identity and Access Management (IAM)** helps you securely control access to AWS resources for your users. Use IAM to control who can use your AWS resources (authentication), what resources they can use, and how they can use them (authorization). For more information, see Authentication and Access Control for Amazon CloudWatch Events.

- **Amazon Kinesis Data Streams** enables rapid and nearly continuous data intake and aggregation. The type of data used includes IT infrastructure log data, application logs, social media, market data feeds, and web clickstream data. Because the response time for the data intake and processing is in real time, processing is typically lightweight. For more information, see the Amazon Kinesis Data Streams Developer Guide.

- **AWS Lambda** enables you to build applications that respond quickly to new information. Upload your application code as Lambda functions and Lambda runs your code on high-availability compute infrastructure. Lambda performs all the administration of the compute resources, including server and operating system maintenance, capacity provisioning, automatic scaling, code and security patch deployment, and code monitoring and logging. For more information, see the AWS Lambda Developer Guide.

CloudWatch Events Limits

CloudWatch Events has the following limits:

Resource	Default Limit
API requests	Up to 50 requests per second for all CloudWatch Events API operations except PutEvents. PutEvents is limited to 400 requests per second by default.
Default event bus	There is no limit on the rate of events that can be received from AWS services or other AWS accounts. If you send custom events to your event bus using the `PutEvents` API, the `PutEvents` API limits apply. Any events that are sent on to the targets of the rules in your account count against your invocations limit. The policy size of the default event bus is limited to 10240 characters. This policy size increases each time you grant access to another account. You can see your current policy and its size by using the `DescribeEventBus` API. You can request a limit increase. For instructions, see AWS Service Limits.
Event pattern	2048 characters maximum.
Invocations	An invocation is an event matching a rule and being sent on to the rule's targets. The limit is 750 per second (after 750 invocations, the invocations are throttled; that is, they still happen but they are delayed). If the invocation of a target fails due to a problem with the target service, account throttling, etc., new attempts are made for up to 24 hours for a specific invocation. If you are receiving events from another account, each of those events that matches a rule in your account and is sent on to the rule's targets counts against your account's limit of 750 invocations per second. You can request a limit increase. For instructions, see AWS Service Limits.
ListRuleNamesByTarget	Up to 100 results per page for requests.
ListRules	Up to 100 results per page for requests.
ListTargetsByRule	Up to 100 results per page for requests.
PutEvents	10 entries per request and 360 requests per second. Each request can be up to 256 KB in size. You can request a limit increase. For instructions, see AWS Service Limits.
PutTargets	10 entries per request.
RemoveTargets	10 entries per request.

Resource	Default Limit
Rules	100 per region per account. You can request a limit increase. For instructions, see AWS Service Limits. Before requesting a limit increase, examine your rules. You may have multiple rules each matching to very specific events. Consider broadening their scope by using fewer identifiers in your Event Patterns in CloudWatch Events. In addition, a rule can invoke several targets each time it matches an event. Consider adding more targets to your rules.
Systems Manager Run Command target	1 target key and 1 target value Systems Manager Run Command does not currently support multiple target values.
Targets	5 per rule.

Setting Up Amazon CloudWatch Events

To use Amazon CloudWatch Events you need an AWS account. Your AWS account allows you to use services (for example, Amazon EC2) to generate events that you can view in the CloudWatch console, a web-based interface. In addition, you can install and configure the AWS Command Line Interface (AWS CLI) to use a command-line interface.

Sign Up for Amazon Web Services (AWS)

When you create an AWS account, we automatically sign up your account for all AWS services. You pay only for the services that you use.

If you have an AWS account already, skip to the next step. If you don't have an AWS account, use the following procedure to create one.

To sign up for an AWS account

1. Open https://aws.amazon.com/, and then choose **Create an AWS Account**. **Note**
   This might be unavailable in your browser if you previously signed into the AWS Management Console. In that case, choose **Sign in to a different account**, and then choose **Create a new AWS account**.

2. Follow the online instructions.

   Part of the sign-up procedure involves receiving a phone call and entering a PIN using the phone keypad.

Sign in to the Amazon CloudWatch Console

To sign in to the Amazon CloudWatch console

1. Sign in to the AWS Management Console and open the CloudWatch console at https://console.aws.amazon.com/cloudwatch/.

2. If necessary, change the region. From the navigation bar, choose the region where you have your AWS resources.

3. In the navigation pane, choose **Events**.

Account Credentials

Although you can use your root user credentials to access CloudWatch Events, we recommend that you use an AWS Identity and Access Management (IAM) account. If you're using an IAM account to access CloudWatch, you must have the following permissions:

```
1  {
2    "Version": "2012-10-17",
3    "Statement": [
4      {
5        "Action": [
6          "events:*",
7          "iam:PassRole"
8        ],
9        "Effect": "Allow",
10       "Resource": "*"
11     }
12   ]
13 }
```

For more information, see Authentication.

Set Up the Command Line Interface

You can use the AWS CLI to perform CloudWatch Events operations.

For information about how to install and configure the AWS CLI, see Getting Set Up with the AWS Command Line Interface in the *AWS Command Line Interface User Guide*.

Regional Endpoints

You must enable regional endpoints (the default) in order to use CloudWatch Events. For more information, see Activating and Deactivating AWS STS in an AWS Region in the *IAM User Guide*.

Getting Started with Amazon CloudWatch Events

Use the procedures in this section to create and delete CloudWatch Events rules. These are general procedures usable for any event source or target. For tutorials written for specific scenarios and specific targets, see Tutorials.

Topics

- Creating a Rule That Triggers On an Event
- Creating a Rule That Triggers On an AWS API Call via CloudTrail
- Creating a Rule That Triggers On a Schedule
- Deleting or Disabling a Rule

Limits

- Some target types might not be available in every region. For more information, see Regions and Endpoints in the *Amazon Web Services General Reference.*

- Creating rules with built-in targets is supported only in the AWS Management Console.

- Amazon SQS FIFO (first-in-first-out) queues are not supported.

- If you create a rule with an encrypted Amazon SQS queue as a target, you must have the following section included in your KMS key policy for the event to be successfully delivered to the encrypted queue.

```
1  {
2              "Sid": "Allow CWE to use the key",
3              "Effect": "Allow",
4              "Principal": {
5                          "Service": "events.amazonaws.com"
6              },
7              "Action": [
8                          "kms:Decrypt",
9                          "kms:GenerateDataKey"
10             ],
11             "Resource": "*"
12 }
```

Creating a CloudWatch Events Rule That Triggers on an Event

Use the following steps to create a CloudWatch Events rule that triggers on an event emitted by an AWS service.

To create a rule that triggers on an event:

1. Open the CloudWatch console at https://console.aws.amazon.com/cloudwatch/.

2. In the navigation pane, choose **Events**, **Create rule**.

3. For **Event source**, do the following:

    1. Choose **Event Pattern**, **Build event pattern to match events by service**.

    2. For **Service Name**, choose the service that emits the event that should to trigger the rule.

    3. For **Event Type**, choose the specific event that is to trigger the rule. If the only option is ** AWS API Call via CloudTrail**, the selected service does not emit events and you can only base rules on API calls made to this service. For more information about creating this type of rule, see Creating a CloudWatch Events Rule That Triggers on an AWS API Call Using AWS CloudTrail.

    4. Depending on the service emitting the event, you may see options for **Any...** and **Specific....** Choose **Any...** to have the event trigger on any type of the selected event, or choose **Specific...** to choose one or more specific event types.

4. For **Targets**, choose **Add Target**, then choose the AWS service that is to act when an event of the selected type is detected.

5. In the other fields in this section, enter information specific to this target type, if any is needed.

6. For many target types, CloudWatch Events needs permission to send events to the target. In these cases, CloudWatch Events can create the IAM role needed for your event to run:

    • To create an IAM role automatically, choose **Create a new role for this specific resource.**
    • To use an IAM role that you created before, choose **Use existing role.**

7. Optionally, repeat steps 4-6 to add another target for this rule.

8. Choose **Configure details**. For **Rule definition**, type a name and description for the rule.

9. Choose **Create rule**.

Creating a CloudWatch Events Rule That Triggers on an AWS API Call Using AWS CloudTrail

To create a rule that triggers on an action by an AWS service that does not emit events, you can base the rule on API calls made by that service, which are recorded by AWS CloudTrail. CloudTrail generally detects all AWS API calls except those calls that begin with Get, List, or Describe. For a complete list of APIs you can use as triggers for rules, see Services Supported by CloudTrail Event History.

To create a rule that triggers on an API call via CloudTrail:

1. Open the CloudWatch console at https://console.aws.amazon.com/cloudwatch/.

2. In the navigation pane, choose **Events, Create rule**.

3. For **Event source**, do the following:

    1. Choose **Event Pattern, Build event pattern to match events by service**.

    2. For **Service Name**, choose the service that uses the API operations to use as the trigger.

    3. For **Event Type**, choose **AWS API Call via CloudTrail**.

    4. To trigger your rule when any API operation for this service is called, choose **Any operation**. To trigger your rule only when certain API operations are called, choose **Specific operation(s)**, type the name of an operation in the next box, and press ENTER. To add more operations, choose **+**.

4. For **Targets**, choose **Add Target**, then choose the AWS service that is to act when an event of the selected type is detected.

5. In the other fields in this section, enter information specific to this target type, if any is needed.

6. For many target types, CloudWatch Events needs permission to send events to the target. In these cases, CloudWatch Events can create the IAM role needed for your event to run:

    - To create an IAM role automatically, choose **Create a new role for this specific resource.**
    - To use an IAM role that you created before, choose **Use existing role**.

7. Optionally, repeat steps 4-6 to add another target for this rule.

8. Choose **Configure details**. For **Rule definition**, type a name and description for the rule.

9. Choose **Create rule**.

Creating a CloudWatch Events Rule That Triggers on a Schedule

Use the following steps to create a CloudWatch Events rule that triggers on a regular schedule.

To create the a rule that triggers on a regular schedule

1. Open the CloudWatch console at https://console.aws.amazon.com/cloudwatch/.

2. In the navigation pane, choose **Events**, **Create rule**.

3. For **Event source**, choose **Schedule**.

4. Choose **Fixed rate of** and specify how often the task is to run, or choose **Cron expression** and specify a cron expression that defines when the task is to be triggered. For more information about cron expression syntax, see Schedule Expressions for Rules.

5. For **Targets**, choose **Add Target**, then choose the AWS service that is to act when an event of the selected type is detected.

6. In the other fields in this section, enter information specific to this target type, if any is needed.

7. For many target types, CloudWatch Events needs permission to send events to the target. In these cases, CloudWatch Events can create the IAM role needed for your event to run:

   - To create an IAM role automatically, choose **Create a new role for this specific resource**.
   - To use an IAM role that you created before, choose **Use existing role**.

8. Optionally, repeat steps 5-7 to add another target for this rule.

9. Choose **Configure details**. For **Rule definition**, type a name and description for the rule.

10. Choose **Create rule**.

Deleting or Disabling a CloudWatch Events Rule

Use the following steps to delete or disable a CloudWatch Events.

To delete or disable a rule

1. Open the CloudWatch console at https://console.aws.amazon.com/cloudwatch/.

2. In the navigation pane, choose **Rules**.

3. Do one of the following:

    1. To delete a rule, select the button next to the rule and choose **Actions**, **Delete**, **Delete**.

    2. To temporarily disable a rule, select the button next to the rule and choose **Actions**, **Disable**, **Disable**.

CloudWatch Events Tutorials

The following tutorials show you how to create CloudWatch Events rules for certain tasks and targets.

Topics

- Tutorial: Relay Events to Amazon EC2 Run Command
- Tutorial: Log EC2 Instance States
- Tutorial: Log Auto Scaling Group States
- Tutorial: Log S3 Object Level Operations
- Tutorial: Use Input Transformer to Customize What is Passed to the Event Target
- Tutorial: Log AWS API Calls
- Tutorial: Schedule Automated EBS Snapshots
- Tutorial: Schedule Lambda Functions
- Tutorial: Set Systems Manager Automation as a Target
- Tutorial: Relay Events to a Kinesis Stream
- Tutorial: Schedule Automated Builds Using AWS CodeBuild

Tutorial: Use CloudWatch Events to Relay Events to Amazon EC2 Run Command

You can use Amazon CloudWatch Events to invoke AWS Systems Manager Run Command and perform actions on Amazon EC2 instances when certain events happen. In this tutorial, set up Run Command to run shell commands and configure each new instance that is launched in an Amazon EC2 Auto Scaling group. This tutorial assumes that you have already assigned a tag to the Amazon EC2 Auto Scaling group, with `environment` as the key and `production` as the value.

To create the CloudWatch Events rule

1. Open the CloudWatch console at https://console.aws.amazon.com/cloudwatch/.

2. In the navigation pane, choose **Events, Create rule**.

3. For **Event source**, do the following:

    1. Choose **Event Pattern, Build event pattern to match events by service**.

    2. For **Service Name**, choose **Auto Scaling**. For **Event Type**, choose **Instance Launch and Terminate**.

    3. Choose **Specific instance event(s)**, **EC2 Instance-launch Lifecycle Action**.

    4. By default, the rule matches any Amazon EC2 Auto Scaling group in the region. To make the rule match a specific group, choose **Specific group name(s)** and then select one or more groups.

    http://docs.aws.amazon.com/AmazonCloudWatch/latest/events/images/cwe_tutorial_runcmd1.P

4. For **Targets**, choose **Add Target, SSM Run Command.**

5. For **Document**, choose **AWS-RunShellScript (Linux)**. (Note that there are many other **Document** options which cover both Linux and Windows instances.) For **Target key**, type **tag:environment**. For **Target value(s)**, type **production** and choose **Add**.

6. Under **Configure parameter(s)**, choose **Constant**.

7. For **Commands**, type a shell command and choose **Add**. Repeat this step for all commands to run when an instance launches.

8. If necessary, type the appropriate information in **WorkingDirectory** and **ExecutionTimeout**.

9. CloudWatch Events can create the IAM role needed for your event to run:

    - To create an IAM role automatically, choose **Create a new role for this specific resource.**
    - To use an IAM role that you created before, choose **Use existing role**.

    http://docs.aws.amazon.com/AmazonCloudWatch/latest/events/images/cwe_tutorial_runcmd2.P

10. Choose **Configure details**. For **Rule definition**, type a name and description for the rule.

11. Choose **Create rule**.

Tutorial: Log the State of an Amazon EC2 Instance Using Cloud-Watch Events

You can create a AWS Lambda function that logs the changes in state for an Amazon EC2 instance. You can choose to create a rule that runs the function whenever there is a state transition or a transition to one or more states that are of interest. In this tutorial, you log the launch of any new instance.

Step 1: Create an AWS Lambda Function

Create a Lambda function to log the state change events. You specify this function when you create your rule.

To create a Lambda function

1. Open the AWS Lambda console at https://console.aws.amazon.com/lambda/.

2. If you are new to Lambda, you see a welcome page; choose **Get Started Now**; otherwise, choose **Create a Lambda function**.

3. On the **Select blueprint** page, type `hello` for the filter, and then choose the **hello-world** blueprint.

4. On the **Configure triggers** page, choose **Next**.

5. On the **Configure function** page, do the following:

    1. Type a name and description for the Lambda function. (For example, name the function "LogEC2InstanceStateChange".)

    2. Edit the sample code for the Lambda function. For example:

    ```
    1 'use strict';
    2
    3 exports.handler = (event, context, callback) => {
    4     console.log('LogEC2InstanceStateChange');
    5     console.log('Received event:', JSON.stringify(event, null, 2));
    6     callback(null, 'Finished');
    7 };
    ```

    3. For **Role**, choose **Choose an existing role** and then choose your basic execution role from **Existing role**. Otherwise, create a new basic execution role.

    4. Choose **Next**.

6. On the **Review** page, choose **Create function**.

Step 2: Create a Rule

Create a rule to run your Lambda function whenever you launch an Amazon EC2 instance.

To create a CloudWatch Events rule

1. Open the CloudWatch console at https://console.aws.amazon.com/cloudwatch/.

2. In the navigation pane, choose **Events**, **Create rule**.

3. For **Event source**, do the following:

    1. Choose **Event Pattern**.

    2. Choose **Build event pattern to match events by service**.

    3. Choose **EC2** and then choose **EC2 Instance State-change Notification**.

4. Choose **Specific state(s)** and then choose **Running**.

5. By default, the rule matches any instance in the region. To make the rule match a specific instance, choose **Specific instance(s)** and then choose one or more instances.

```
http://docs.aws.amazon.com/AmazonCloudWatch/latest/events/images/log_stateec2_using_CWE
```

4. For **Targets**, choose **Add target** and then choose **Lambda function**.

5. For **Function**, select the Lambda function that you created.

6. Choose **Configure details**.

7. For **Rule definition**, type a name and description for the rule.

8. Choose **Create rule**.

Step 3: Test the Rule

To test your rule, launch an Amazon EC2 instance. After waiting a few minutes for the instance to launch and initialize, you can verify that your Lambda function was invoked.

To test your rule by launching an instance

1. Open the Amazon EC2 console at https://console.aws.amazon.com/ec2/.

2. Launch an instance. For more information, see Launch Your Instance in the *Amazon EC2 User Guide for Linux Instances*.

3. Open the CloudWatch console at https://console.aws.amazon.com/cloudwatch/.

4. In the navigation pane, choose **Events**, **Rules**, select the name of the rule that you created, and choose**Show metrics for the rule**.

5. To view the output from your Lambda function, do the following:

   1. In the navigation pane, choose **Logs**.

   2. Choose the name of the log group for your Lambda function (/aws/lambda/*function-name*).

   3. Choose the name of log stream to view the data provided by the function for the instance that you launched.

6. (Optional) When you are finished, you can open the Amazon EC2 console and stop or terminate the instance that you launched. For more information, see Terminate Your Instance in the *Amazon EC2 User Guide for Linux Instances*.

Tutorial: Log the State of an Auto Scaling Group Using CloudWatch Events

You can run an AWS Lambda function that logs an event whenever an Auto Scaling group launches or terminates an Amazon EC2 instance and whether the launch or terminate event was successful.

For additional CloudWatch Events scenarios using Auto Scaling events, see Getting CloudWatch Events When Your Auto Scaling Group Scales in the *Amazon EC2 Auto Scaling User Guide*.

Step 1: Create an AWS Lambda Function

Create a Lambda function to log the scale out and scale in events for your Auto Scaling group. You specify this function when you create your rule.

To create a Lambda function

1. Open the AWS Lambda console at https://console.aws.amazon.com/lambda/.

2. If you are new to Lambda, you see a welcome page; choose **Get Started Now**; otherwise, choose **Create a Lambda function**.

3. On the **Select blueprint** page, type `hello` for the filter, and then choose the **hello-world** blueprint.

4. On the **Configure triggers** page, choose **Next**.

5. On the **Configure function** page, do the following:

   1. Type a name and description for the Lambda function. (For example, name the function "LogAutoScalingEvent".)

   2. Edit the sample code for the Lambda function. For example:

   ```
   1 'use strict';
   2
   3 exports.handler = (event, context, callback) => {
   4     console.log('LogAutoScalingEvent');
   5     console.log('Received event:', JSON.stringify(event, null, 2));
   6     callback(null, 'Finished');
   7 };
   ```

   3. For **Role**, choose **Choose an existing role** and then choose your basic execution role from **Existing role**. Otherwise, create a new basic execution role.

   4. Choose **Next**.

6. Choose **Create function**.

Step 2: Create a Rule

Create a rule to run your Lambda function whenever your Auto Scaling group launches or terminates an instance.

To create a rule

1. Open the CloudWatch console at https://console.aws.amazon.com/cloudwatch/.

2. In the navigation pane, choose **Events**, **Create rule**.

3. For **Event source**, do the following:

   1. Choose **Event Pattern**.

2. Choose **Build event pattern to match events by service.**

3. Choose **Auto Scaling** and then choose **Instance Launch and Terminate.**

4. Choose **Any instance event** to capture all successful and unsuccessful instance launch and terminate events.

http://docs.aws.amazon.com/AmazonCloudWatch/latest/events/images/log_stateautoscaling1.

4. By default, the rule matches any Auto Scaling group in the region. To make the rule match a specific Auto Scaling group, choose **Specific group name(s)** and then choose one or more Auto Scaling groups.

5. For **Targets**, choose **Add target** and then choose **Lambda function.**

6. For **Function**, select the Lambda function that you created.

7. Choose **Configure details.**

8. For **Rule definition**, type a name and description for the rule. (For example, describe the rule as "Log whenever an Auto Scaling group scales out or in".)

9. Choose **Create rule.**

Step 3: Test the Rule

You can test your rule by manually scaling an Auto Scaling group so that it launches an instance. After waiting a few minutes for the scale out event to occur, you can verify that your Lambda function was invoked.

To test your rule using an Auto Scaling group

1. To increase the size of your Auto Scaling group, do the following:

   1. Open the Amazon EC2 console at https://console.aws.amazon.com/ec2/.

   2. On the navigation pane, choose **Auto Scaling, Auto Scaling Groups.**

   3. Select the check box for your Auto Scaling group.

   4. On the **Details** tab, choose **Edit.** For **Desired**, increase the desired capacity by one. For example, if the current value is 2, type 3. The desired capacity must be less than or equal to the maximum size of the group. Therefore, you must update **Max** if your new value for **Desired** is greater than **Max.** When you are finished, choose **Save.**

2. Open the CloudWatch console at https://console.aws.amazon.com/cloudwatch/.

3. In the navigation pane, choose **Events, Rules**, select the name of the rule that you created, and then choose **Show metrics for the rule.**

4. To view the output from your Lambda function, do the following:

   1. In the navigation pane, choose **Logs.**

   2. Select the name of the log group for your Lambda function (/aws/lambda/*function-name*).

   3. Select the name of log stream to view the data provided by the function for the instance that you launched.

5. (Optional) When you are finished, you can decrease the desired capacity by one so that the Auto Scaling group returns to its previous size.

Tutorial: Log Amazon S3 Object-Level Operations Using Cloud-Watch Events

You can log the object-level API operations on your S3 buckets. Before Amazon CloudWatch Events can match these events, you must use AWS CloudTrail to set up a trail configured to receive these events.

Step 1: Configure Your AWS CloudTrail Trail

To log data events for an S3 bucket to AWS CloudTrail and CloudWatch Events, create a trail. A trail captures API calls and related events in your account and delivers the log files to an S3 bucket that you specify. You can update an existing trail or create a new one.

To create a trail

1. Open the CloudTrail console at https://console.aws.amazon.com/cloudtrail/.

2. In the navigation pane, choose **Trails, Create trail**.

3. For **Trail name**, type a name for the trail.

4. For **Data events,** type the bucket name and prefix (optional). For each trail, you can add up to 250 Amazon S3 objects.

   - To log data events for all Amazon S3 objects in a bucket, specify an S3 bucket and an empty prefix. When an event occurs on an object in that bucket, the trail processes and logs the event.
   - To log data events for specific Amazon S3 objects, specify an S3 bucket and the object prefix. When an event occurs on an object in that bucket and the object starts with the specified prefix, the trail processes and logs the event.

5. For each resource, specify whether to log **Read-only**, **Write-only**, or **All** events.

6. For **Storage location**, create or choose an existing S3 bucket to designate for log file storage.

7. Choose **Create**.

For more information, see Data Events in the AWS CloudTrail User Guide.

Step 2: Create an AWS Lambda Function

Create a Lambda function to log data events for your S3 buckets. You specify this function when you create your rule.

To create a Lambda function

1. Open the AWS Lambda console at https://console.aws.amazon.com/lambda/.

2. If you are new to Lambda, you see a welcome page; choose **Get Started Now**; otherwise, choose **Create a Lambda function**.

3. On the **Select blueprint** page, type `hello` for the filter, and then choose the **hello-world** blueprint.

4. On the **Configure triggers** page, choose **Next**.

5. On the **Configure function** page, do the following:

   1. Type a name and description for the Lambda function. (For example, name the function "LogS3DataEvents".)

   2. Edit the code for the Lambda function. For example:

```
1 'use strict';
2
3 exports.handler = (event, context, callback) => {
4     console.log('LogS3DataEvents');
5     console.log('Received event:', JSON.stringify(event, null, 2));
6     callback(null, 'Finished');
7 };
```

   3. For **Role**, choose **Choose an existing role** and then choose your basic execution role from **Existing role**. Otherwise, create a new basic execution role.

   4. Choose **Next**.

6. On the **Review** page, choose **Create function**.

Step 3: Create a Rule

Create a rule to run your Lambda function in response to an Amazon S3 data event.

To create a rule

1. Open the CloudWatch console at https://console.aws.amazon.com/cloudwatch/.

2. In the navigation pane, choose **Events**, **Create rule**.

3. For **Event source**, do the following:

   1. Choose **Event Pattern**.

   2. Choose **Build event pattern to match events by service**.

   3. Choose **Simple Storage Service (S3)** and then choose **Object Level Operations**.

   4. Choose **Specific operation(s)** and then choose **PutObject**.

   5. By default, the rule matches data events for all buckets in the region. To match data events for specific buckets, choose **Specify bucket(s) by name** and then specify one or more buckets.

`http://docs.aws.amazon.com/AmazonCloudWatch/latest/events/images/log_state_S3PutObject.`

4. For **Targets**, choose **Add target**, and then choose **Lambda function**.

5. For **Function**, select the Lambda function that you created.

6. Choose **Configure details**.

7. For **Rule definition**, type a name and description for the rule.

8. Choose **Create rule**.

Step 4: Test the Rule

To test the rule, put an object in your S3 bucket. You can verify that your Lambda function was invoked.

To view the logs for your Lambda function

1. Open the CloudWatch console at https://console.aws.amazon.com/cloudwatch/.

2. In the navigation pane, choose **Logs**.

3. Select the name of the log group for your Lambda function (/aws/lambda/*function-name*).

4. Select the name of log stream to view the data provided by the function for the instance that you launched.

You can also check the contents of your CloudTrail logs in the S3 bucket that you specified for your trail. For more information, see Getting and Viewing Your CloudTrail Log Files in the *AWS CloudTrail User Guide.*

Tutorial: Use Input Transformer to Customize What is Passed to the Event Target

You can use the input transformer feature of CloudWatch Events to customize the text that is taken from an event before it is input to the target of a rule.

You can define multiple JSON paths from the event and assign their outputs to different variables. Then you can use those variables in the input template in the form of <*variable-name*>.

If you specify a variable to match a JSON path that does not exist in the event, the variable is replaced with null. The characters < and > cannot be escaped.

In this tutorial, we extract the instance-id and state of an Amazon EC2 instance from the instance state change event. We use input transformer to put that data into an easy-to-read message that is sent to an Amazon SNS topic. The rule is triggered when any instance changes to any state. For example, with this rule, the following Amazon EC2 instance state-change notification event produces the Amazon SNS message **The EC2 instance i-1234567890abcdef0 has changed state to stopped.**

```
1  {
2      "id":"7bf73129-1428-4cd3-a780-95db273d1602",
3      "detail-type":"EC2 Instance State-change Notification",
4      "source":"aws.ec2",
5      "account":"123456789012",
6      "time":"2015-11-11T21:29:54Z",
7      "region":"us-east-1",
8      "resources":[
9          "arn:aws:ec2:us-east-1:123456789012:instance/ i-1234567890abcdef0"
10     ],
11     "detail":{
12         "instance-id":" i-1234567890abcdef0",
13         "state":"stopped"
14     }
15 }
```

We achieve this by mapping the *instance* variable to the $.detail.instance-id JSON path from the event, and the *state* variable to the $.detail.state JSON path. We then set the input template as "The EC2 instance has changed state to ."

Create a Rule

To use input transformer to customize Amazon EC2 instance state change information that is sent to a target

1. Open the CloudWatch console at https://console.aws.amazon.com/cloudwatch/.

2. In the navigation pane, choose **Events, Create rule**.

3. For **Event source**, do the following:

    1. Choose **Event Pattern**.

    2. Choose **Build event pattern to match events by service**.

    3. Choose **EC2** and then choose **EC2 Instance State-change Notification**.

    4. Choose **Any state** and **Any instance**.

4. For **Targets**, choose **Add target** and then choose **SNS topic**.

5. For **Topic**, select the Amazon SNS topic that you want to be notified when Amazon EC2 instances change state.

6. Choose **Configure input, Input Transformer**.

7. In the next box, type **{"state" : "$.detail.state", "instance" : "$.detail.instance-id"}**

8. In the following box, type **"The EC2 instance has changed state to ."**

9. Choose **Configure details**.

10. Type a name and description for the rule, and choose **Create rule**.

Tutorial: Log AWS API Calls Using CloudWatch Events

You can use a AWS Lambda function that logs each AWS API call. For example, you can create a rule to log any operation within Amazon EC2, or you can limit this rule to log only a specific API call. In this tutorial, you log every time an Amazon EC2 instance is stopped.

Prerequisite

Before you can match these events, you must use AWS CloudTrail to set up a trail. If you do not have a trail, complete the following procedure.

To create a trail

1. Open the CloudTrail console at https://console.aws.amazon.com/cloudtrail/.

2. Choose **Trails**, **Add new trail**.

3. For **Trail name**, type a name for the trail.

4. For **S3 bucket**, type the name for the new bucket where CloudTrail will deliver logs.

5. Choose **Create**.

Step 1: Create an AWS Lambda Function

Create a Lambda function to log the API call events. You specify this function when you create your rule.

To create a Lambda function

1. Open the AWS Lambda console at https://console.aws.amazon.com/lambda/.

2. If you are new to Lambda, you see a welcome page; choose **Get Started Now**; otherwise, choose **Create a Lambda function**.

3. On the **Select blueprint** page, type `hello` for the filter, and then choose the **hello-world** blueprint.

4. On the **Configure triggers** page, choose **Next**.

5. On the **Configure function** page, do the following:

   1. Type a name and description for the Lambda function. (For example, name the function "LogEC2StopInstance".)

   2. Edit the sample code for the Lambda function. For example:

   ```
   1  'use strict';
   2
   3  exports.handler = (event, context, callback) => {
   4      console.log('LogEC2StopInstance');
   5      console.log('Received event:', JSON.stringify(event, null, 2));
   6      callback(null, 'Finished');
   7  };
   ```

   3. For **Role**, choose **Choose an existing role** and then choose your basic execution role from **Existing role**. Otherwise, create a new basic execution role.

   4. Choose **Next**.

6. On the **Review** page, choose **Create function**.

Step 2: Create a Rule

Create a rule to run your Lambda function whenever you stop an Amazon EC2 instance.

To create a rule

1. Open the CloudWatch console at https://console.aws.amazon.com/cloudwatch/.

2. In the navigation pane, choose **Events**, **Create rule**.

3. Choose .

4. For **Event source**, do the following:

    1. Choose **Event Pattern**.

    2. Choose **Build event pattern to match events by service**.

    3. Choose **EC2** and then choose **AWS API Call via CloudTrail**.

    4. Choose **Specific operation(s)** and then type StopInstances in the box below.

5. For **Targets**, choose **Add target** and then choose **Lambda function**.

6. For **Function**, select the Lambda function that you created.

7. Choose **Configure details**.

8. For **Rule definition**, type a name and description for the rule.

9. Choose **Create rule**.

Step 3: Test the Rule

You can test your rule by stopping an Amazon EC2 instance using the Amazon EC2 console. After waiting a few minutes for the instance to stop, check your AWS Lambda metrics in the CloudWatch console to verify that your function was invoked.

To test your rule by stopping an instance

1. Open the Amazon EC2 console at https://console.aws.amazon.com/ec2/.

2. Launch an instance. For more information, see Launch Your Instance in the *Amazon EC2 User Guide for Linux Instances*.

3. Stop the instance. For more information, see Stop and Start Your Instance in the *Amazon EC2 User Guide for Linux Instances*.

4. Open the CloudWatch console at https://console.aws.amazon.com/cloudwatch/.

5. In the navigation pane, choose **Events**, select the name of the rule that you created, and choose **Show metrics for the rule**.

6. To view the output from your Lambda function, do the following:

    1. In the navigation pane, choose **Logs**.

    2. Select the name of the log group for your Lambda function (/aws/lambda/*function-name*).

    3. Select the name of log stream to view the data provided by the function for the instance that you stopped.

7. (Optional) When you are finished, you can terminate the stopped instance. For more information, see Terminate Your Instance in the *Amazon EC2 User Guide for Linux Instances*.

Tutorial: Schedule Automated Amazon EBS Snapshots Using CloudWatch Events

You can run CloudWatch Events rules according to a schedule. In this tutorial, you create an automated snapshot of an existing Amazon Elastic Block Store (Amazon EBS) volume on a schedule. You can choose a fixed rate to create a snapshot every few minutes or use a cron expression to specify that the snapshot is made at a specific time of day.

Important
Creating rules with built-in targets is supported only in the AWS Management Console.

Step 1: Create a Rule

Create a rule that takes snapshots on a schedule. You can use a rate expression or a cron expression to specify the schedule. For more information, see Schedule Expressions for Rules.

To create a rule

1. Open the CloudWatch console at https://console.aws.amazon.com/cloudwatch/.

2. In the navigation pane, choose **Events**, **Create rule**.

3. For **Event Source**, do the following:

   1. Choose **Schedule**.

   2. Choose **Fixed rate of** and specify the schedule interval (for example, 5 minutes). Alternatively, choose **Cron expression** and specify a cron expression (for example, every 15 minutes Monday through Friday, starting at the current time).

4. For **Targets**, choose **Add target** and then select **EC2 Create Snapshot API call**.

5. For **Volume ID**, type the volume ID of the targeted Amazon EBS volume.

6. For **AWS permissions**, choose the option to create a new role. The new role grants the built-in target permissions to access resources on your behalf.

7. Choose **Configure details**.

8. For **Rule definition**, type a name and description for the rule.

9. Choose **Create rule**.

Step 2: Test the Rule

You can verify your rule by viewing your first snapshot after it is taken.

To test your rule

1. Open the Amazon EC2 console at https://console.aws.amazon.com/ec2/.

2. In the navigation pane, choose **Elastic Block Store**, **Snapshots**.

3. Verify that the first snapshot appears in the list.

4. (Optional) When you are finished, you can disable the rule to prevent additional snapshots from being taken.

   1. Open the CloudWatch console at https://console.aws.amazon.com/cloudwatch/.

   2. In the navigation pane, choose **Events**, **Rules**.

3. Select the rule and then choose **Actions**, **Disable**.

4. When prompted for confirmation, choose **Disable**.

Tutorial: Schedule AWS Lambda Functions Using CloudWatch Events

You can set up a rule to run an AWS Lambda function on a schedule. This tutorial shows how to use the AWS Management Console or the AWS CLI to create the rule. If you would like to use the AWS CLI but have not installed it, see the AWS Command Line Interface User Guide.

CloudWatch Events does not provide second-level precision in schedule expressions. The finest resolution using a cron expression is a minute. Due to the distributed nature of the CloudWatch Events and the target services, the delay between the time the scheduled rule is triggered and the time the target service honors the execution of the target resource might be several seconds. Your scheduled rule is triggered within that minute but not on the precise 0th second.

Step 1: Create an AWS Lambda Function

Create a Lambda function to log the scheduled events. You specify this function when you create your rule.

To create a Lambda function

1. Open the AWS Lambda console at https://console.aws.amazon.com/lambda/.

2. If you are new to Lambda, you see a welcome page; choose **Get Started Now**; otherwise, choose **Create a Lambda function**.

3. On the **Select blueprint** page, type `hello` for the filter, and then choose the **hello-world** blueprint.

4. On the **Configure triggers** page, choose **Next**.

5. On the **Configure function** page, do the following:

   1. Type a name and description for the Lambda function. (For example, name the function "LogScheduledEvent".)

   2. Edit the sample code for the Lambda function. For example:

```
1  'use strict';
2
3  exports.handler = (event, context, callback) => {
4      console.log('LogScheduledEvent');
5      console.log('Received event:', JSON.stringify(event, null, 2));
6      callback(null, 'Finished');
7  };
```

   3. For **Role**, choose **Choose an existing role** and then choose your basic execution role from **Existing role**. Otherwise, create a new basic execution role.

   4. Choose **Next**.

6. On the **Review** page, choose **Create function**.

Step 2: Create a Rule

Create a rule to run your Lambda function on a schedule.

To create a rule using the console

1. Open the CloudWatch console at https://console.aws.amazon.com/cloudwatch/.

2. In the navigation pane, choose **Events**, **Create rule**.

3. For **Event Source**, do the following:

   1. Choose **Schedule**.

   2. Choose **Fixed rate of** and specify the schedule interval (for example, 5 minutes).

4. For **Targets**, choose **Add target** and then choose **Lambda function**.

5. For **Function**, select the Lambda function that you created.

6. Choose **Configure details**.

7. For **Rule definition**, type a name and description for the rule.

8. Choose **Create rule**.

If you prefer, you can create the rule using the AWS CLI. First, you must grant the rule permission to invoke your Lambda function. Then you can create the rule and add the Lambda function as a target.

To create a rule using the AWS CLI

1. Use the following put-rule command to create a rule that triggers itself on a schedule:

```
1 aws events put-rule \
2 --name my-scheduled-rule \
3 --schedule-expression 'rate(5 minutes)'
```

   When this rule triggers, it generates an event that serves as input to the targets of this rule. The following is an example event:

```
1 {
2     "version": "0",
3     "id": "53dc4d37-cffa-4f76-80c9-8b7d4a4d2eaa",
4     "detail-type": "Scheduled Event",
5     "source": "aws.events",
6     "account": "123456789012",
7     "time": "2015-10-08T16:53:06Z",
8     "region": "us-east-1",
9     "resources": [
10         "arn:aws:events:us-east-1:123456789012:rule/my-scheduled-rule"
11     ],
12     "detail": {}
13 }
```

2. Use the following add-permission command to trust the CloudWatch Events service principal (events.amazonaws.com) and scope permissions to the rule with the specified Amazon Resource Name (ARN):

```
1 aws lambda add-permission \
2 --function-name LogScheduledEvent \
3 --statement-id my-scheduled-event \
4 --action 'lambda:InvokeFunction' \
5 --principal events.amazonaws.com \
6 --source-arn arn:aws:events:us-east-1:123456789012:rule/my-scheduled-rule
```

3. Use the following put-targets command to add the Lambda function that you created to this rule so that it runs every five minutes:

```
1 aws events put-targets --rule my-scheduled-rule --targets file://targets.json
```

   Create the file **targets.json** with the following contents:

```
1 [
2   {
3     "Id": "1",
4     "Arn": "arn:aws:lambda:us-east-1:123456789012:function:LogScheduledEvent"
5   }
6 ]
```

Step 3: Test the Rule

You can verify that your Lambda function was invoked.

To test your rule

1. Open the CloudWatch console at https://console.aws.amazon.com/cloudwatch/.

2. In the navigation pane, choose **Events**, **Rules**, select the name of the rule that you created, and choose **Show metrics for the rule**.

3. To view the output from your Lambda function, do the following:

   1. In the navigation pane, choose **Logs**.

   2. Select the name of the log group for your Lambda function (/aws/lambda/*function-name*).

   3. Select the name of log stream to view the data provided by the function for the instance that you launched.

4. (Optional) When you are finished, you can disable the rule.

   1. Open the CloudWatch console at https://console.aws.amazon.com/cloudwatch/.

   2. In the navigation pane, choose **Events**, **Rules**.

   3. Select the rule and then choose **Actions**, **Disable**.

   4. When prompted for confirmation, choose **Disable**.

Tutorial: Set AWS Systems Manager Automation as a CloudWatch Events Target

You can use CloudWatch Events to invoke AWS Systems Manager Automation on a regular timed schedule, or when specified events are detected. This tutorial assumes you are invoking Systems Manager Automation based on certain events.

To create the CloudWatch Events rule

1. Open the CloudWatch console at https://console.aws.amazon.com/cloudwatch/.

2. In the navigation pane, choose **Events, Create rule.**

3. For **Event source**, do the following:

   1. Choose **Event Pattern** and choose **Build event pattern to match events by service.**

   2. For **Service Name** and **Event Type**, choose the service and event type to use as the trigger.

      Depending on the service and event type you choose, you may need to specify additional options under **Event Source.**

4. For **Targets**, choose **Add Target, SSM Automation.**

5. For **Document**, choose the Systems Manager document to run when the target is triggered.

6. (Optional), To specify a certain version of the document, choose **Configure document version.**

7. Under **Configure parameter(s)**, choose **No Parameter(s)** or **Constant.**

   If you choose **Constant**, specify the constants to pass to the document execution.

8. CloudWatch Events can create the IAM role needed for your event to run:

   - To create an IAM role automatically, choose **Create a new role for this specific resource.**
   - To use an IAM role that you created before, choose **Use existing role.**

9. Choose **Configure details**. For **Rule definition**, type a name and description for the rule.

10. Choose **Create rule.**

Tutorial: Relay Events to an Amazon Kinesis Stream Using Cloud-Watch Events

You can relay AWS API call events in CloudWatch Events to a stream in Amazon Kinesis.

Prerequisite

Install the AWS CLI. For more information, see the AWS Command Line Interface User Guide.

Step 1: Create an Amazon Kinesis Stream

Use the following create-stream command to create a stream.

```
1 aws kinesis create-stream --stream-name test --shard-count 1
```

When the stream status is `ACTIVE`, the stream is ready. Use the following describe-stream command to check the stream status:

```
1 aws kinesis describe-stream --stream-name test
```

Step 2: Create a Rule

As an example, create a rule to send events to your stream when you stop an Amazon EC2 instance.

To create a rule

1. Open the CloudWatch console at https://console.aws.amazon.com/cloudwatch/.

2. In the navigation pane, choose **Events**, **Create rule**.

3. For **Event source**, do the following:

    1. Choose **Event Pattern**.

    2. Choose **Build event pattern to match events by service**.

    3. Choose **EC2** and then choose **Instance State-change Notification**.

    4. Choose **Specific state(s)** and then choose **Running**.

4. For **Targets**, choose **Add target**, and then choose **Kinesis stream**.

5. For **Stream**, select the stream that you created.

6. Choose **Create a new role for this specific resource**.

7. Choose **Configure details**.

8. For **Rule definition**, type a name and description for the rule.

9. Choose **Create rule**.

Step 3: Test the Rule

To test your rule, stop an Amazon EC2 instance. After waiting a few minutes for the instance to stop, check your CloudWatch metrics to verify that your function was invoked.

To test your rule by stopping an instance

1. Open the Amazon EC2 console at https://console.aws.amazon.com/ec2/.

2. Launch an instance. For more information, see Launch Your Instance in the *Amazon EC2 User Guide for Linux Instances*.

3. Open the CloudWatch console at https://console.aws.amazon.com/cloudwatch/.

4. In the navigation pane, choose **Events**, **Rules**, select the name of the rule that you created, and choose **Show metrics for the rule**.

5. (Optional) When you are finished, you can terminate the instance. For more information, see Terminate Your Instance in the *Amazon EC2 User Guide for Linux Instances*.

Step 4: Verify That the Event is Relayed

You can get the record from the stream to verify that the event was relayed.

To get the record

1. Use the following get-shard-iterator command to start reading from your Kinesis stream:

```
1 aws kinesis get-shard-iterator --shard-id shardId-000000000000 --shard-iterator-type
    TRIM_HORIZON --stream-name test
```

The following is example output:

```
1 {
2     "ShardIterator": "AAAAAAAAAAHSywljvOzEgPX4NyKdZ5wryMzP9yALs8NeKbUjp1IxtZs1Sp+
        KEd9I6AJ9ZG4lNR1EMi+9Md/nHvtLyxpfhEzYvkTZ4D9DQVz/mBYWRO6OTZRKnW9gd+
        efGN2aHFdkH1rJ14BL9Wyrk+ghYG22D2T1Da2EyNSH1+LAbK33gQweTJADBdyMwlo5r6PqcP2dzhg="
3 }
```

2. Use the following get-records command to get the record. The shard iterator is the one you got in the previous step:

```
1 aws kinesis get-records --shard-iterator
    AAAAAAAAAAHSywljvOzEgPX4NyKdZ5wryMzP9yALs8NeKbUjp1IxtZs1Sp+KEd9I6AJ9ZG4lNR1EMi+9Md/
    nHvtLyxpfhEzYvkTZ4D9DQVz/mBYWRO6OTZRKnW9gd+efGN2aHFdkH1rJ14BL9Wyrk+ghYG22D2T1Da2EyNSH1+
    LAbK33gQweTJADBdyMwlo5r6PqcP2dzhg=
```

If the command is successful, it requests records from your stream for the specified shard. You can receive zero or more records. Any records returned might not represents all records in your stream. If you don't receive the data you expect, keep calling `get-records`.

Records in Kinesis are Base64-encoded. However, the streams support in the AWS CLI does not provide Base64 decoding. If you use a Base64 decoder to manually decode the data, you see that it is the event relayed to the stream in JSON form.

Tutorial: Schedule Automated Builds Using AWS CodeBuild

In the example in this tutorial, you schedule AWS CodeBuild to run a build every weeknight at 8pm GMT. You also pass a constant to AWS CodeBuild to be used for this scheduled build.

To create a rule scheduling a AWS CodeBuild project build nightly at 8pm

1. Open the CloudWatch console at https://console.aws.amazon.com/cloudwatch/.

2. In the navigation pane, choose **Events**, **Create rule**.

3. For **Event Source**, do the following:

    1. Choose **Schedule**.

    2. Choose **Cron expression** and specify the the following as the expression: **0 20 ? * MON-FRI ***. For more information about cron expressions, see Schedule Expressions for Rules.

4. For **Targets**, choose **Add target** and then select **CodeBuild project**.

5. For **Project ARN**, type the ARN of the build project.

6. In this tutorial, we add the optional step of passing a parameter to AWS CodeBuild, to override the default. This is not required when you set AWS CodeBuild as the target. To pass the parameter, choose **Configure input**, **Constant (JSON text)**.

    In the box under **Constant (JSON text)**, type the following to set the timeout override to 30 minutes for these scheduled builds: **{ "timeoutInMinutesOverride": 30 }**

    For more information about the parameters you can pass, see StartBuild. You cannot pass the `projectName` parameter in this field. Instead, you specify the project using the ARN in **Project ARN**.

7. CloudWatch Events can create the IAM role needed for your build project to run:

    - To create an IAM role automatically, choose **Create a new role for this specific resource.**
    - To use an IAM role that you created before, choose **Use existing role**. This must be a role that already has sufficient permissions to invoke the build. CloudWatch Events does not grant additional permissions to the role you select.

8. Choose **Configure details**

9. For **Rule definition**, type a name and description for the rule.

10. Choose **Create rule**.

Schedule Expressions for Rules

You can create rules that self-trigger on an automated schedule in CloudWatch Events using cron or rate expressions. All scheduled events use UTC time zone and the minimum precision for schedules is 1 minute.

CloudWatch Events does not provide second-level precision in schedule expressions. The finest resolution using a cron expression is a minute. Due to the distributed nature of the CloudWatch Events and the target services, the delay between the time the scheduled rule is triggered and the time the target service honors the execution of the target resource might be several seconds. Your scheduled rule is triggered within that minute, but not on the precise 0th second.

CloudWatch Events supports the following formats for schedule expressions.

Topics

- Cron Expressions
- Rate Expressions

Cron Expressions

Cron expressions have six required fields, which are separated by white space.

Syntax

```
1 cron(fields)
```

Field	Values	Wildcards
Minutes	0-59	, - * /
Hours	0-23	, - * /
Day-of-month	1-31	, - * ? / L W
Month	1-12 or JAN-DEC	, - * /
Day-of-week	1-7 or SUN-SAT	, - * ? L #
Year	1970-2199	, - * /

Wildcards

- The **,** (comma) wildcard includes additional values. In the Month field, JAN,FEB,MAR would include January, February, and March.
- The **-** (dash) wildcard specifies ranges. In the Day field, 1-15 would include days 1 through 15 of the specified month.
- The ***** (asterisk) wildcard includes all values in the field. In the Hours field, ***** would include every hour.
- The **/** (forward slash) wildcard specifies increments. In the Minutes field, you could enter 1/10 to specify every tenth minute, starting from the first minute of the hour (for example, the 11th, 21st, and 31st minute, and so on).
- The **?** (question mark) wildcard specifies one or another. In the Day-of-month field you could enter **7** and if you didn't care what day of the week the 7th was, you could enter **?** in the Day-of-week field.
- The **L** wildcard in the Day-of-month or Day-of-week fields specifies the last day of the month or week.
- The **W** wildcard in the Day-of-month field specifies a weekday. In the Day-of-month field, 3W specifies the day closest to the third weekday of the month.
- The **#** wildcard in the Day-of-week field specifies a certain instance of the specified day of the week within a month. For example, 3#2 would be the second Tuesday of the month: the 3 refers to Tuesday because it is the third day of each week, and the 2 refers to the second day of that type within the month.

Limits

- You can't specify the Day-of-month and Day-of-week fields in the same cron expression. If you specify a value (or a *) in one of the fields, you must use a **?** (question mark) in the other.
- Cron expressions that lead to rates faster than 1 minute are not supported.

Examples

You can use the following sample cron strings when creating a rule with schedule.

Minutes	Hours	Day of month	Month	Day of week	Year	Meaning
0	10	*	*	?	*	Run at 10:00 am (UTC) every day
15	12	*	*	?	*	Run at 12:15 pm (UTC) every day
0	18	?	*	MON-FRI	*	Run at 6:00 pm (UTC) every Monday through Friday
0	8	1	*	?	*	Run at 8:00 am (UTC) every 1st day of the month
0/15	*	*	*	?	*	Run every 15 minutes
0/10	*	?	*	MON-FRI	*	Run every 10 minutes Monday through Friday
0/5	8-17	?	*	MON-FRI	*	Run every 5 minutes Monday through Friday between 8:00 am and 5:55 pm (UTC)

The following examples show how to use Cron expressions with the AWS CLI put-rule command. The first example creates a rule that is triggered every day at 12:00pm UTC.

```
1 aws events put-rule --schedule-expression "cron(0 12 * * ? *)" --name MyRule1
```

The next example creates a rule that is triggered every day, at 5 and 35 minutes past 2:00pm UTC.

```
1 aws events put-rule --schedule-expression "cron(5,35 14 * * ? *)" --name MyRule2
```

The next example creates a rule that is triggered at 10:15am UTC on the last Friday of each month during the years 2002 to 2005.

```
1 aws events put-rule --schedule-expression "cron(15 10 ? * 6L 2002-2005)" --name MyRule3
```

Rate Expressions

A rate expression starts when you create the scheduled event rule, and then runs on its defined schedule.

Rate expressions have two required fields. Fields are separated by white space.

Syntax

```
1 rate(value unit)
```

value
A positive number.

unit
The unit of time.
Valid values: minute | minutes | hour | hours | day | days

Limits
If the value is equal to 1, then the unit must be singular. Similarly, for values greater than 1, the unit must be plural. For example, rate(1 hours) and rate(5 hour) are not valid, but rate(1 hour) and rate(5 hours) are valid.

Examples
The following examples show how to use rate expressions with the AWS CLI put-rule command.

```
1 aws events put-rule --schedule-expression "rate(5 minutes)" --name MyRule3
```

```
1 aws events put-rule --schedule-expression "rate(1 hour)" --name MyRule4
```

```
1 aws events put-rule --schedule-expression "rate(1 day)" --name MyRule5
```

Event Patterns in CloudWatch Events

Events in Amazon CloudWatch Events are represented as JSON objects. For more information about JSON objects, see RFC 7159. The following is an example event:

```
1  {
2    "version": "0",
3    "id": "6a7e8feb-b491-4cf7-a9f1-bf3703467718",
4    "detail-type": "EC2 Instance State-change Notification",
5    "source": "aws.ec2",
6    "account": "111122223333",
7    "time": "2015-12-22T18:43:48Z",
8    "region": "us-east-1",
9    "resources": [
10     "arn:aws:ec2:us-east-1:123456789012:instance/i-12345678"
11   ],
12   "detail": {
13     "instance-id": "i-12345678",
14     "state": "terminated"
15   },
16   "StatusMessage": ""
17 }
```

It is important to remember the following details about an event:

- They all have the same top-level fields – the ones appearing in the example above – which are never absent.
- The contents of the **detail** top-level field are different depending on which service generated the event and what the event is. The combination of the **source** and **detail-type** fields serves to identify the fields and values found in the **detail** field. For examples of events generated by AWS services, see Event Types for CloudWatch Events.

Each event field is described below.

version
By default, this is set to 0 (zero) in all events.

id
A unique value is generated for every event. This can be helpful in tracing events as they move through rules to targets, and are processed.

detail-type
Identifies, in combination with the **source** field, the fields and values that appear in the **detail** field.

source
Identifies the service that sourced the event. All events sourced from within AWS begin with "aws." Customer-generated events can have any value here, as long as it doesn't begin with "aws." We recommend the use of Java package-name style reverse domain-name strings.
To find the correct value for `source` for an AWS service, see the table in AWS Service Namespaces. For example, the `source` value for Amazon CloudFront is `aws.cloudfront`.

account
The 12-digit number identifying an AWS account.

time
The event timestamp, which can be specified by the service originating the event. If the event spans a time interval, the service might choose to report the start time, so this value can be noticeably before the time the event is actually received.

43

region

Identifies the AWS region where the event originated.

resources

This JSON array contains ARNs that identify resources that are involved in the event. Inclusion of these ARNs is at the discretion of the service. For example, Amazon EC2 instance state-changes include Amazon EC2 instance ARNs, Auto Scaling events include ARNs for both instances and Auto Scaling groups, but API calls with AWS CloudTrail do not include resource ARNs.

detail

A JSON object, whose content is at the discretion of the service originating the event. The detail content in the example above is very simple, just two fields. AWS API call events have detail objects with around 50 fields nested several levels deep.

Event Patterns

Rules use event patterns to select events and route them to targets. A pattern either matches an event or it doesn't. Event patterns are represented as JSON objects with a structure that is similar to that of events, for example:

```
1 {
2   "source": [ "aws.ec2" ],
3   "detail-type": [ "EC2 Instance State-change Notification" ],
4   "detail": {
5     "state": [ "running" ]
6   }
7 }
```

It is important to remember the following about event pattern matching:

- For a pattern to match an event, the event must contain all the field names listed in the pattern. The field names must appear in the event with the same nesting structure.
- Other fields of the event not mentioned in the pattern are ignored; effectively, there is a ”*”: ”*” wildcard for fields not mentioned.
- The matching is exact (character-by-character), without case-folding or any other string normalization.
- The values being matched follow JSON rules: Strings enclosed in quotes, numbers, and the unquoted keywords `true`, `false`, and `null`.
- Number matching is at the string representation level. For example, 300, 300.0, and 3.0e2 are not considered equal.

When you write patterns to match events, you can use the `TestEventPattern` API or the `test-event-pattern` CLI command to make sure that your pattern will match the desired events. For more information, see TestEventPattern or test-event-pattern.

The following event patterns would match the event at the top of this page. The first pattern matches because one of the instance values specified in the pattern matches the event (and the pattern does not specify any additional fields not contained in the event). The second one matches because the ”terminated” state is contained in the event.

```
1 {
2   "resources": [
3     "arn:aws:ec2:us-east-1:123456789012:instance/i-12345678",
4     "arn:aws:ec2:us-east-1:123456789012:instance/i-abcdefgh"
5   ]
6 }
```

```
1 {
2   "detail": {
3     "state": [ "terminated" ]
4   }
5 }
```

These event patterns do not match the event at the top of this page. The first pattern does not match because the pattern specifies a "pending" value for state, and this value does not appear in the event. The second pattern does not match because the resource value specified in the pattern does not appear in the event.

```
1 {
2   "source": [ "aws.ec2" ],
3   "detail-type": [ "EC2 Instance State-change Notification" ],
4   "detail": {
5     "state": [ "pending" ]
6   }
7 }
```

```
1 {
2   "source": [ "aws.ec2" ],
3   "detail-type": [ "EC2 Instance State-change Notification" ],
4   "resources": [ "arn:aws:ec2:us-east-1::image/ami-12345678" ]
5 }
```

Matching Null Values and Empty Strings In Event Patterns

You can create a pattern that matches an event field that has a null value or an empty string. To see how this works, consider the following example event:

```
1 {
2   "version": "0",
3   "id": "3e3c153a-8339-4e30-8c35-687ebef853fe",
4   "detail-type": "EC2 Instance Launch Successful",
5   "source": "aws.autoscaling",
6   "account": "123456789012",
7   "time": "2015-11-11T21:31:47Z",
8   "region": "us-east-1",
9   "resources": [
10   ],
11   "detail": {
12     "eventVersion": "",
13     "responseElements": null
14   }
15 }
```

To match events where the value of `eventVersion` is an empty string, use the following pattern, which would match the event example.

```
1 {
2   "detail": {
3     "eventVersion": [""]
4   }
5 }
```

To match events where the value of `responseElements` is null, use the following pattern, which would match the event example.

```
1 {
2   "detail": {
3       "responseElements": [null]
4   }
5 }
```

Null values and empty strings are not interchangeable in patttern matching. A pattern that is written to detect empty strings will not catch values of `null`.

Arrays In CloudWatch Events Patterns

The value of each field in a pattern is an array containing one or more values, and the pattern matches if any of the values in the array match the value in the event. If the value in the event is an array, then the pattern matches if the intersection of the pattern array and the event array is non-empty.

For example, an example event pattern includes the following text:

```
1 "resources": [
2     "arn:aws:ec2:us-east-1:123456789012:instance/i-b188560f",
3     "arn:aws:ec2:us-east-1:111122223333:instance/i-b188560f",
4     "arn:aws:ec2:us-east-1:444455556666:instance/i-b188560f",
5 ]
```

The example pattern would match an event that includes the following text, because the first item in the pattern array matches the second item in the event array.

```
1 "resources": [
2     "arn:aws:autoscaling:us-east-1:123456789012:autoScalingGroup:eb56d16b-bbf0-401d-b893-
           d5978ed4a025:autoScalingGroupName/ASGTerminate",
3     "arn:aws:ec2:us-east-1:123456789012:instance/i-b188560f"
4 ]
```

CloudWatch Events Event Examples From Each Supported Service

The following AWS services emit events that can be detected by CloudWatch Events:

Topics

- Events for Services Not Listed
- Auto Scaling Events
- AWS API Call Events
- AWS Batch Events
- AWS CodeBuild Events
- AWS CodeCommit Events
- AWS CodeDeploy Events
- AWS CodePipeline Events
- AWS Management Console Sign-in Events
- Amazon EBS Events
- Amazon EC2 Events
- AWS OpsWorks Stacks Events
- AWS Systems Manager Events
- AWS Systems Manager Parameter Store Events
- AWS Systems Manager Configuration Compliance Events
- Amazon EC2 Maintenance Windows Events
- Amazon ECS Events
- Amazon EMR Events
- Amazon GameLift Event
- AWS Glue Events
- Amazon GuardDuty Events
- AWS Health Events
- AWS KMS Events
- Amazon Macie Events
- Scheduled Events
- AWS Server Migration Service Events
- AWS Trusted Advisor Events

Events for Services Not Listed

You can also use CloudWatch Events with services that do not emit events and are not on the preceding list. AWS CloudTrail is a service that automatically records events such as AWS service API calls. You can create CloudWatch Events rules that trigger on the information captured by CloudTrail. For more information about CloudTrail, see What is AWS CloudTrail?. For more information about creating a CloudWatch Events rule that uses CloudTrail, see Creating a CloudWatch Events Rule That Triggers on an AWS API Call Using AWS CloudTrail.

Auto Scaling Events

The following are examples of the events for Auto Scaling. For more information, see Getting CloudWatch Events When Your Auto Scaling Group Scales in the *Amazon EC2 Auto Scaling User Guide*.

EC2 Instance-launch Lifecycle Action

Auto Scaling moved an instance to a `Pending:Wait` state due to a lifecycle hook.

```
1  {
2    "version": "0",
3    "id": "6a7e8feb-b491-4cf7-a9f1-bf3703467718",
```

```json
    "detail-type": "EC2 Instance-launch Lifecycle Action",
    "source": "aws.autoscaling",
    "account": "123456789012",
    "time": "2015-12-22T18:43:48Z",
    "region": "us-east-1",
    "resources": [
      "arn:aws:autoscaling:us-east-1:123456789012:autoScalingGroup:59fcbb81-bd02-485d-80ce-563
          ef5b237bf:autoScalingGroupName/sampleASG"
    ],
    "detail": {
      "LifecycleActionToken": "c613620e-07e2-4ed2-a9e2-ef8258911ade",
      "AutoScalingGroupName": "my-asg",
      "LifecycleHookName": "my-lifecycle-hook",
      "EC2InstanceId": "i-1234567890abcdef0",
      "LifecycleTransition": "autoscaling:EC2_INSTANCE_LAUNCHING",
      "NotificationMetadata": "additional-info"
    }
}
```

EC2 Instance Launch Successful

Auto Scaling successfully launched an instance.

```json
{
  "id": "3e3c153a-8339-4e30-8c35-687ebef853fe",
  "detail-type": "EC2 Instance Launch Successful",
  "source": "aws.autoscaling",
  "account": "123456789012",
  "time": "2015-11-11T21:31:47Z",
  "region": "us-east-1",
  "resources": [
      "arn:aws:autoscaling:us-east-1:123456789012:autoScalingGroup:eb56d16b-bbf0-401d-b893-
          d5978ed4a025:autoScalingGroupName/ASGLaunchSuccess",
      "arn:aws:ec2:us-east-1:123456789012:instance/i-b188560f"
      ],
  "detail": {
      "StatusCode": "InProgress",
      "AutoScalingGroupName": "ASGLaunchSuccess",
      "ActivityId": "9cabb81f-42de-417d-8aa7-ce16bf026590",
      "Details": {
            "Availability Zone": "us-east-1b",
            "Subnet ID": "subnet-95bfcebe"
      },
      "RequestId": "9cabb81f-42de-417d-8aa7-ce16bf026590",
      "EndTime": "2015-11-11T21:31:47.208Z",
      "EC2InstanceId": "i-b188560f",
      "StartTime": "2015-11-11T21:31:13.671Z",
      "Cause": "At 2015-11-11T21:31:10Z a user request created an Auto Scaling group changing
          the desired capacity from 0 to 1. At 2015-11-11T21:31:11Z an instance was started in
          response to a difference between desired and actual capacity, increasing the capacity
          from 0 to 1."
    }
}
```

EC2 Instance Launch Unsuccessful

Auto Scaling failed to launch an instance.

```
1  {
2    "id": "1681ab87-4a09-459f-95a2-7fa09403c4b7",
3    "detail-type": "EC2 Instance Launch Unsuccessful",
4    "source": "aws.autoscaling",
5    "account": "123456789012",
6    "time": "2015-11-11T21:42:36Z",
7    "region": "us-east-1",
8    "resources": [
9        "arn:aws:autoscaling:us-east-1:123456789012:autoScalingGroup:528ffce5-ef9f-4c1d-8d18-5
            d005b4a438c:autoScalingGroupName/brokenASG",
10       "arn:aws:ec2:us-east-1:123456789012:instance/"
11       ],
12   "detail": {
13       "StatusCode": "Failed",
14       "AutoScalingGroupName": "brokenASG",
15       "ActivityId": "06076c51-4874-487d-b15b-7895a713ab55",
16       "Details": {
17           "Availability Zone": "us-east-1e",
18           "Subnet ID": "subnet-16c5df2c"
19       },
20       "RequestId": "06076c51-4874-487d-b15b-7895a713ab55",
21       "EndTime": "2015-11-11T21:42:36.000Z",
22       "EC2InstanceId": "",
23       "StartTime": "2015-11-11T21:42:36.698Z",
24       "Cause": "At 2015-11-11T21:42:09Z a user request update of Auto Scaling group constraints
            to min: 0, max: 10, desired: 2 changing the desired capacity from 0 to 2. At
            2015-11-11T21:42:35Z an instance was started in response to a difference between
            desired and actual capacity, increasing the capacity from 0 to 2."
25       }
26 }
```

EC2 Instance-terminate Lifecycle Action

Auto Scaling moved an instance to a Terminating:Wait state due to a lifecycle hook.

```
1  {
2    "version": "0",
3    "id": "468fe059-f4b7-445f-bb22-2a271b94974d",
4    "detail-type": "EC2 Instance-terminate Lifecycle Action",
5    "source": "aws.autoscaling",
6    "account": "123456789012",
7    "time": "2015-12-22T18:43:48Z",
8    "region": "us-east-1",
9    "resources": [
10     "arn:aws:autoscaling:us-east-1:123456789012:autoScalingGroup:59fcbb81-bd02-485d-80ce-563
            ef5b237bf:autoScalingGroupName/sampleASG"
11   ],
12   "detail": {
13     "LifecycleActionToken": "630aa23f-48eb-45e7-aba6-799ea6093a0f",
14     "AutoScalingGroupName": "sampleASG",
15     "LifecycleHookName": "SampleLifecycleHook-6789",
16     "EC2InstanceId": "i-12345678",
17     "LifecycleTransition": "autoscaling:EC2_INSTANCE_TERMINATING"
18   }
```

```
19  }
```

EC2 Instance Terminate Successful

Auto Scaling successfully terminated an instance.

```
1  {
2    "id": "156d01c9-a6c3-4d7e-b883-5758266b95af",
3    "detail-type": "EC2 Instance Terminate Successful",
4    "source": "aws.autoscaling",
5    "account": "123456789012",
6    "time": "2015-11-11T21:36:57Z",
7    "region": "us-east-1",
8    "resources": [
9        "arn:aws:autoscaling:us-east-1:123456789012:autoScalingGroup:eb56d16b-bbf0-401d-b893-
              d5978ed4a025:autoScalingGroupName/ASGTerminate",
10       "arn:aws:ec2:us-east-1:123456789012:instance/i-b188560f"
11       ],
12   "detail": {
13       "StatusCode": "InProgress",
14       "AutoScalingGroupName": "ASGTerminate",
15       "ActivityId": "56472e79-538a-4ba7-b3cc-768d889194b0",
16       "Details": {
17           "Availability Zone": "us-east-1b",
18           "Subnet ID": "subnet-95bfcebe"
19           },
20       "RequestId": "56472e79-538a-4ba7-b3cc-768d889194b0",
21       "EndTime": "2015-11-11T21:36:57.498Z",
22       "EC2InstanceId": "i-b188560f",
23       "StartTime": "2015-11-11T21:36:12.649Z",
24       "Cause": "At 2015-11-11T21:36:03Z a user request update of Auto Scaling group constraints
              to min: 0, max: 1, desired: 0 changing the desired capacity from 1 to 0. At 2015-11-11
              T21:36:12Z an instance was taken out of service in response to a difference between
              desired and actual capacity, shrinking the capacity from 1 to 0. At 2015-11-11T21
              :36:12Z instance i-b188560f was selected for termination."
25       }
26  }
```

EC2 Instance Terminate Unsuccessful

Auto Scaling failed to terminate an instance.

```
1  {
2    "id": "5e3df53a-0239-4e31-7d15-087ebef903ce",
3    "detail-type": "EC2 Instance Terminate Unsuccessful",
4    "source": "aws.autoscaling",
5    "account": "123456789012",
6    "time": "2015-12-01T23:34:57Z",
7    "region": "us-east-1",
8    "resources": [
9        "arn:aws:autoscaling:us-east-1:123456789012:autoScalingGroup:cf5ebd9c-8e2a-4197-abe2-2
              fb94e8d1f87:autoScalingGroupName/ASGTermFail",
10       "arn:aws:ec2:us-east-1:123456789012:instance/i-b188560f"
11       ],
12   "detail": {
13       "StatusCode": "InProgress",
14       "Description": "Terminating EC2 instance: i-b188560f",
```

```
15      "AutoScalingGroupName": "ASGTermFail",
16      "ActivityId": "c1a8f6ce-82e8-4517-96ba-67d1999ceee4",
17      "Details": {
18           "Availability Zone": "us-east-1e",
19           "Subnet ID": "subnet-915643ba"
20           },
21      "RequestId": "c1a8f6ce-82e8-4517-96ba-67d1999ceee4",
22      "StatusMessage": "",
23      "EndTime": "2015-12-01T23:34:57.721Z",
24      "EC2InstanceId": "i-b188560f",
25      "StartTime": "2015-12-01T23:33:48.489Z",
26      "Cause": "At 2015-12-01T23:33:41Z a user request explicitly set group desired capacity
            changing the desired capacity from 2 to 0. At 2015-12-01T23:33:47Z an instance was
            taken out of service in response to a difference between desired and actual capacity,
            shrinking the capacity from 2 to 0. At 2015-12-01T23:33:47Z instance i-0867
            b4292c0cff474 was selected for termination. At 2015-12-01T23:33:48Z instance i-
            b188560f was selected for termination."
27      }
28 }
```

AWS API Call Events

The following is an example of an AWS API call event to Amazon S3 to create a bucket:

```
1  {
2      "version": "0",
3      "id": "36eb8523-97d0-4518-b33d-ee3579ff19f0",
4      "detail-type": "AWS API Call via CloudTrail",
5      "source": "aws.s3",
6      "account": "123456789012",
7      "time": "2016-02-20T01:09:13Z",
8      "region": "us-east-1",
9      "resources": [],
10     "detail": {
11        "eventVersion": "1.03",
12        "userIdentity": {
13           "type": "Root",
14           "principalId": "123456789012",
15           "arn": "arn:aws:iam::123456789012:root",
16           "accountId": "123456789012",
17           "sessionContext": {
18              "attributes": {
19                 "mfaAuthenticated": "false",
20                 "creationDate": "2016-02-20T01:05:59Z"
21              }
22           }
23        },
24        "eventTime": "2016-02-20T01:09:13Z",
25        "eventSource": "s3.amazonaws.com",
26        "eventName": "CreateBucket",
27        "awsRegion": "us-east-1",
28        "sourceIPAddress": "100.100.100.100",
29        "userAgent": "[S3Console/0.4]",
30        "requestParameters": {
```

```
31          "bucketName": "bucket-test-iad"
32        },
33        "responseElements": null,
34        "requestID": "9D767BCC3B4E7487",
35        "eventID": "24ba271e-d595-4e66-a7fd-9c16cbf8abae",
36        "eventType": "AwsApiCall"
37      }
38 }
```

Only the read/write events from the following services are supported. Read-only operations—such as those that begin with **List**, **Get**, or **Describe**—aren't supported. In addition, AWS API call events that are larger than 256 KB in size are not supported.

- Amazon EC2 Auto Scaling
- AWS Certificate Manager
- AWS CloudFormation
- Amazon CloudFront
- AWS CloudHSM
- Amazon CloudSearch
- AWS CloudTrail
- Amazon CloudWatch
- Amazon CloudWatch Events
- Amazon CloudWatch Logs
- AWS CodeDeploy
- AWS CodePipeline
- Amazon Cognito Identity
- Amazon Cognito Sync
- AWS Config
- AWS Data Pipeline
- AWS Device Farm
- AWS Direct Connect
- AWS Directory Service
- AWS Database Migration Service
- Amazon DynamoDB
- Amazon Elastic Container Registry
- Amazon Elastic Container Service
- Amazon EC2 Systems Manager
- Amazon ElastiCache
- AWS Elastic Beanstalk
- Amazon Elastic Compute Cloud
- Amazon Elastic File System
- Elastic Load Balancing
- Amazon EMR
- Amazon Elastic Transcoder
- Amazon Elasticsearch Service
- Amazon GameLift
- Amazon Glacier
- AWS Identity and Access Management [US East (N. Virginia) only]
- Amazon Inspector
- AWS IoT
- AWS Key Management Service
- Amazon Kinesis
- Amazon Kinesis Data Firehose
- AWS Lambda
- Amazon Machine Learning

- AWS OpsWorks
- Amazon Polly
- Amazon Redshift
- Amazon Relational Database Service
- Amazon Route 53
- AWS Security Token Service
- Amazon Simple Email Service
- Amazon Simple Notification Service
- Amazon Simple Queue Service
- Amazon Simple Storage Service
- Amazon Simple Workflow Service
- AWS Step Functions
- AWS Storage Gateway
- AWS Support
- AWS WAF
- Amazon WorkDocs
- Amazon WorkSpaces

AWS Batch Events

For examples of events generated by AWS Batch, see AWS Batch Events.

AWS CodeBuild Events

For AWS CodeBuild sample events, see Build Notifications Input Format Reference in the *AWS CodeBuild User Guide*.

AWS CodeCommit Events

The following are examples of events for AWS CodeCommit.

referenceCreated event

```
{
    "version": "0",
    "id": "01234567-0123-0123-0123-012345678901",
    "detail-type": "CodeCommit Repository State Change",
    "source": "aws.codecommit",
    "account": "123456789012",
    "time": "2017-06-12T10:23:43Z",
    "region": "us-east-1",
    "resources": [
      "arn:aws:codecommit:us-east-1:123456789012:myRepo"
    ],
    "detail": {
      "event": "referenceCreated",
      "repositoryName": "myRepo",
      "repositoryId": "12345678-1234-5678-abcd-12345678abcd",
      "referenceType": "tag",
      "referenceName": "myTag",
      "referenceFullName": "refs/tags/myTag",
      "commitId": "3e5983EXAMPLE"
    }
```

```
21  }
```

referenceUpdated event

```
1  {
2       "version": "0",
3       "id": "01234567-0123-0123-0123-012345678901",
4       "detail-type": "CodeCommit Repository State Change",
5       "source": "aws.codecommit",
6       "account": "123456789012",
7       "time": "2017-06-12T10:23:43Z",
8       "region": "us-east-1",
9       "resources": [
10        "arn:aws:codecommit:us-east-1:123456789012:myRepo"
11      ],
12      "detail": {
13        "event": "referenceUpdated",
14        "repositoryName": "myRepo",
15        "repositoryId": "12345678-1234-5678-abcd-12345678abcd",
16        "referenceType": "branch",
17        "referenceName": "myBranch",
18        "referenceFullName": "refs/heads/myBranch",
19        "commitId": "26a8f2EXAMPLE",
20        "oldCommitId": "3e5983EXAMPLE"
21      }
22  }
```

referenceDeleted event

```
1  {
2       "version": "0",
3       "id": "01234567-0123-0123-0123-012345678901",
4       "detail-type": "CodeCommit Repository State Change",
5       "source": "aws.codecommit",
6       "account": "123456789012",
7       "time": "2017-06-12T10:23:43Z",
8       "region": "us-east-1",
9       "resources": [
10        "arn:aws:codecommit:us-east-1:123456789012:myRepo"
11      ],
12      "detail": {
13        "event": "referenceDeleted",
14        "repositoryName": "myRepo",
15        "repositoryId": "12345678-1234-5678-abcd-12345678abcd",
16        "referenceType": "branch",
17        "referenceName": "myBranch",
18        "referenceFullName": "refs/heads/myBranch",
19        "oldCommitId": "26a8f2EXAMPLE"
20      }
21  }
```

AWS CodeDeploy Events

The following are examples of the events for AWS CodeDeploy. For more information, see Monitoring Deployments with CloudWatch Events in the *AWS CodeDeploy User Guide.*

CodeDeploy Deployment State-change Notification

There was a change in the state of a deployment.

```
1  {
2    "account": "123456789012",
3    "region": "us-east-1",
4    "detail-type": "CodeDeploy Deployment State-change Notification",
5    "source": "aws.codedeploy",
6    "version": "0",
7    "time": "2016-06-30T22:06:31Z",
8    "id": "c071bfbf-83c4-49ca-a6ff-3df053957145",
9    "resources": [
10     "arn:aws:codedeploy:us-east-1:123456789012:application:myApplication",
11     "arn:aws:codedeploy:us-east-1:123456789012:deploymentgroup:myApplication/myDeploymentGroup"
12   ],
13   "detail": {
14     "instanceGroupId": "9fd2fbef-2157-40d8-91e7-6845af69e2d2",
15     "region": "us-east-1",
16     "application": "myApplication",
17     "deploymentId": "d-123456789",
18     "state": "SUCCESS",
19     "deploymentGroup": "myDeploymentGroup"
20   }
21 }
```

CodeDeploy Instance State-change Notification

There was a change in the state of an instance that belongs to a deployment group.

```
1  {
2    "account": "123456789012",
3    "region": "us-east-1",
4    "detail-type": "CodeDeploy Instance State-change Notification",
5    "source": "aws.codedeploy",
6    "version": "0",
7    "time": "2016-06-30T23:18:50Z",
8    "id": "fb1d3015-c091-4bf9-95e2-d98521ab2ecb",
9    "resources": [
10     "arn:aws:ec2:us-east-1:123456789012:instance/i-0000000aaaaaaaaaa",
11     "arn:aws:codedeploy:us-east-1:123456789012:deploymentgroup:myApplication/myDeploymentGroup",
12     "arn:aws:codedeploy:us-east-1:123456789012:application:myApplication"
13   ],
14   "detail": {
15     "instanceId": "i-0000000aaaaaaaaaa",
16     "region": "us-east-1",
17     "state": "SUCCESS",
18     "application": "myApplication",
19     "deploymentId": "d-123456789",
20     "instanceGroupId": "8cd3bfa8-9e72-4cbe-a1e5-da4efc7efd49",
21     "deploymentGroup": "myDeploymentGroup"
22   }
23 }
```

AWS CodePipeline Events

The following are examples of events for AWS CodePipeline.

Pipeline Execution State Change

```
1  {
2    "version": "0",
3    "id": "CWE-event-id",
4    "detail-type": "CodePipeline Pipeline Execution State Change",
5    "source": "aws.codepipeline",
6    "account": "123456789012",
7    "time": "2017-04-22T03:31:47Z",
8    "region": "us-east-1",
9    "resources": [
10     "arn:aws:codepipeline:us-east-1:123456789012:pipeline:myPipeline"
11   ],
12   "detail": {
13     "pipeline": "myPipeline",
14     "version": "1",
15     "state": "STARTED",
16     "execution-id": "01234567-0123-0123-0123-012345678901"
17   }
18 }
```

Stage Execution State Change

```
1  {
2    "version": "0",
3    "id": "CWE-event-id",
4    "detail-type": "CodePipeline Stage Execution State Change",
5    "source": "aws.codepipeline",
6    "account": "123456789012",
7    "time": "2017-04-22T03:31:47Z",
8    "region": "us-east-1",
9    "resources": [
10     "arn:aws:codepipeline:us-east-1:123456789012:pipeline:myPipeline"
11   ],
12   "detail": {
13     "pipeline": "myPipeline",
14     "version": "1",
15     "execution-id": "01234567-0123-0123-0123-012345678901",
16     "stage": "Prod",
17     "state": "STARTED"
18   }
19 }
```

Action Execution State Change

```
1  {
2    "version": "0",
3    "id": "CWE-event-id",
4    "detail-type": "CodePipeline Action Execution State Change",
5    "source": "aws.codepipeline",
6    "account": "123456789012",
7    "time": "2017-04-22T03:31:47Z",
8    "region": "us-east-1",
```

```
 9    "resources": [
10      "arn:aws:codepipeline:us-east-1:123456789012:pipeline:myPipeline"
11    ],
12    "detail": {
13      "pipeline": "myPipeline",
14      "version": 1,
15      "execution-id": "01234567-0123-0123-0123-012345678901",
16      "stage": "Prod",
17      "action": "myAction",
18      "state": "STARTED",
19      "type": {
20        "owner": "AWS",
21        "category": "Deploy",
22        "provider": "CodeDeploy",
23        "version": 1
24      }
25    }
26  }
```

AWS Management Console Sign-in Events

The following is an example of a console sign-in event:

```
 1  {
 2    "id": "6f87d04b-9f74-4f04-a780-7acf4b0a9b38",
 3    "detail-type": "AWS Console Sign In via CloudTrail",
 4    "source": "aws.signin",
 5    "account": "123456789012",
 6    "time": "2016-01-05T18:21:27Z",
 7    "region": "us-east-1",
 8    "resources": [],
 9    "detail": {
10        "eventVersion": "1.02",
11        "userIdentity": {
12            "type": "Root",
13            "principalId": "123456789012",
14            "arn": "arn:aws:iam::123456789012:root",
15            "accountId": "123456789012"
16            },
17        "eventTime": "2016-01-05T18:21:27Z",
18        "eventSource": "signin.amazonaws.com",
19        "eventName": "ConsoleLogin",
20        "awsRegion": "us-east-1",
21        "sourceIPAddress": "0.0.0.0",
22        "userAgent": "Mozilla/5.0 (Macintosh; Intel Mac OS X 10_10_5) AppleWebKit/537.36 (KHTML,
                like Gecko) Chrome/47.0.2526.106 Safari/537.36",
23        "requestParameters": null,
24        "responseElements": {
25            "ConsoleLogin": "Success"
26            },
27        "additionalEventData": {
28            "LoginTo": "https://console.aws.amazon.com/console/home?state=hashArgs%23&isauthcode
                    =true",
29            "MobileVersion": "No",
```

```
30        "MFAUsed": "No" },
31      "eventID": "324731c0-64b3-4421-b552-dfc3c27df4f6",
32      "eventType": "AwsConsoleSignIn"
33      }
34 }
```

Amazon EBS Events

The following are examples of the events for Amazon Elastic Block Store (Amazon EBS). For more information, see Amazon CloudWatch Events for Amazon EBS in the *Amazon EC2 User Guide for Linux Instances*.

EBS Snapshot Notification

Amazon EBS created a snapshot (createSnapshot), copied a snapshot (copySnapshot), or shared a snapshot (shareSnapshot). The source field within the detail field does not include the account-id as part of the volume ARN.

```
1  {
2    "version": "0",
3    "id": "01234567-0123-0123-0123-012345678901",
4    "detail-type": "EBS Snapshot Notification",
5    "source": "aws.ec2",
6    "account": "123456789012",
7    "time": "2016-11-14T01:30:00Z",
8    "region": "us-east-1",
9    "resources": [
10     "arn:aws:ec2::us-west-2:snapshot/snap-01234567"
11   ],
12   "detail": {
13     "event": "createSnapshot",
14     "result": "succeeded",
15     "cause": "",
16     "request-id": "",
17     "snapshot_id": "arn:aws:ec2::us-west-2:snapshot/snap-01234567",
18     "source": "arn:aws:ec2::us-west-2:volume/vol-01234567",
19     "StartTime": "2016-11-14T00:00:00Z",
20     "EndTime": "2016-11-ddT01:30:00Z"
21   }
22 }
```

EBS Volume Notification

Events are generated when Amazon EBS creates or deletes a volume, fails to create a volume, fails to attach a volume, or fails to reattach a volume.

Amazon EBS Volume Creation

```
1  {
2    "version":"0",
3    "id":"01234567-0123-0123-0123-0123456789ab",
4    "detail-type":"EBS Volume Notification",
5    "source":"aws.ec2",
6    "account":"0123456789ab",
7    "time":"2017-12-29T17:29:54Z",
8    "region":"us-east-1",
9    "resources":[
```

```
10        "arn:aws:ec2:us-east-1:0123456789ab:volume/vol-01234567"
11      ],
12      "detail":{
13        "result":"available",
14        "cause":"",
15        "event":"createVolume",
16        "request-id":"01234567-0123-0123-0123-0123456789ab"
17      }
18  }
```

Amazon EBS Volume Deletion

```
1  {
2      "version":"0",
3      "id":"01234567-0123-0123-0123-0123456789ab",
4      "detail-type":"EBS Volume Notification",
5      "source":"aws.ec2",
6      "account":"0123456789ab",
7      "time":"2017-12-29T17:28:57Z",
8      "region":"us-east-1",
9      "resources":[
10        "arn:aws:ec2:us-east-1: 0123456789ab:volume/vol-01234567"
11      ],
12      "detail":{
13        "result":"deleted",
14        "cause":"",
15        "event":"deleteVolume",
16        "request-id":"01234567-0123-0123-0123-0123456789ab"
17      }
18  }
```

Amazon EBS Volume Creation Failure

The following example shows a failed attempt to create a volume. Events for failed attach and re-attach are similar, except that the value of the "event" field is attachVolume or reattachVolume in those cases.

```
1  {
2      "version": "0",
3      "id": "01234567-0123-0123-0123-0123456789ab",
4      "detail-type": "EBS Volume Notification",
5      "source": "aws.ec2",
6      "account": "012345678901",
7      "time": "2016-11-14T00:30:07Z",
8      "region": "sa-east-1",
9      "resources": [
10        "arn:aws:ec2:sa-east-1:0123456789ab:volume/vol-01234567",
11      ],
12      "detail": {
13        "event": "createVolume",
14        "result": "failed",
15        "cause": "arn:aws:kms:sa-east-1:0123456789ab:key/01234567-0123-0123-0123-0123456789ab is
                disabled.",
16        "request-id": "01234567-0123-0123-0123-0123456789ab",
17
18  }
```

Amazon EC2 Events

The following are examples of events for Amazon EC2.

EC2 Instance State-change Notification

This example of an EC2 Instance State-change Notification event shows the instance in the `pending` state. The other possible values for `state` include `running`, `shutting-down`, `stopped`, `stopping`, and `terminated`.

```
 1 {
 2     "id":"7bf73129-1428-4cd3-a780-95db273d1602",
 3     "detail-type":"EC2 Instance State-change Notification",
 4     "source":"aws.ec2",
 5     "account":"123456789012",
 6     "time":"2015-11-11T21:29:54Z",
 7     "region":"us-east-1",
 8     "resources":[
 9         "arn:aws:ec2:us-east-1:123456789012:instance/i-abcd1111"
10     ],
11     "detail":{
12         "instance-id":"i-abcd1111",
13         "state":"pending"
14     }
15 }
```

EC2 Spot Instance Interruption

The following is an example of the event emitted when Amazon EC2 interrupts a Spot instance.

```
 1 {
 2     "version": "0",
 3     "id": "12345678-1234-1234-1234-123456789012",
 4     "detail-type": "EC2 Spot Instance Interruption Warning",
 5     "source": "aws.ec2",
 6     "account": "123456789012",
 7     "time": "yyyy-mm-ddThh:mm:ssZ",
 8     "region": "us-east-2",
 9     "resources": ["arn:aws:ec2:us-east-2:123456789012:instance/i-1234567890abcdef0"],
10     "detail": {
11         "instance-id": "i-1234567890abcdef0",
12         "instance-action": "action"
13     }
14 }
```

AWS OpsWorks Stacks Events

The following are examples of AWS OpsWorks Stacks events.

AWS OpsWorks Stacks instance state change

Indicates a change in the state of an AWS OpsWorks Stacks instance. The following are instance states.

- booting
- connection_lost
- online
- pending
- rebooting

- requested
- running_setup
- setup_failed
- shutting_down
- start_failed
- stopping
- stop_failed
- stopped
- terminating
- terminated

```
1  {
2    "version": "0",
3    "id": "dc5fa8df-48f1-2108-b1b9-1fe5ebcf2296",
4    "detail-type": "OpsWorks Instance State Change",
5    "source": "aws.opsworks",
6    "account": "123456789012",
7    "time": "2018-01-25T11:12:23Z",
8    "region": "us-east-1",
9    "resources": [
10     "arn:aws:opsworks:us-east-1:123456789012:instance/a648d98f-fdd8-4323-952a-a50z3e4z500z"
11   ],
12   "detail": {
13     "initiated_by": "user",
14     "hostname": "testing1",
15     "stack-id": "acd3df16-e859-4598-8414-377b12a902da",
16     "layer-ids": [
17       "d1a0cb7f-c7e9-4a63-811c-976f0267b2c8"
18     ],
19     "instance-id": "a648d98f-fdd8-4323-952a-a50z3e4z500z",
20     "ec2-instance-id": "i-08b1c2b67aa292276",
21     "status": "requested"
22   }
23 }
```

The initiated_by field is only populated when the instance is in the requested, terminating, or stopping states. The initiated_by field can contain one of the following values.

- user - A user requested the instance state change by using either the API or AWS Management Console.
- auto-scaling - The AWS OpsWorks Stacks automatic scaling feature initiated the instance state change.
- auto-healing - The AWS OpsWorks Stacks automatic healing feature initiated the instance state change.

AWS OpsWorks Stacks command state change

A change occurred in the state of an AWS OpsWorks Stacks command. The following are command states.

- expired - A command timed out.
- failed - A general command failure occurred.
- skipped - A command was skipped because the instance has a different state in AWS OpsWorks Stacks than in Amazon EC2.
- successful - A command succeeded.
- superseded - A command was skipped because it would have applied configuration changes that have already been applied.

```
1  {
2    "version": "0",
3    "id": "96c778b6-a40e-c8c1-aafc-c9852a3a7b52",
4    "detail-type": "OpsWorks Command State Change",
```

```
 5    "source": "aws.opsworks",
 6    "account": "123456789012",
 7    "time": "2018-01-26T08:54:40Z",
 8    "region": "us-east-1",
 9    "resources": [
10      "arn:aws:opsworks:us-east-1:123456789012:instance/a648d98f-fdd8-4323-952a-a50a3e4e500f"
11    ],
12    "detail": {
13      "command-id": "acc9f4f3-a3ec-4fab-b70f-c7d04e71e3ec",
14      "instance-id": "a648d98f-fdd8-4323-952a-a50a3e4e500f",
15      "type": "setup",
16      "status": "successful"
17    }
18 }
```

AWS OpsWorks Stacks deployment state change

A change occurred in the state of an AWS OpsWorks Stacks deployment. The following are deployment states.

- running
- successful
- failed

```
 1 {
 2    "version": "0",
 3    "id": "b8230afa-60c7-f43f-b632-841c1cfb22ff",
 4    "detail-type": "OpsWorks Deployment State Change",
 5    "source": "aws.opsworks",
 6    "account": "123456789012",
 7    "time": "2018-01-25T11:15:48Z",
 8    "region": "us-east-1",
 9    "resources": [
10      "arn:aws:opsworks:us-east-1:123456789012:instance/a648d98f-fdd8-4323-952a-a50a3e4e500f"
11    ],
12    "detail": {
13      "duration": 16,
14      "stack-id": "acd3df16-e859-4598-8414-377b12a902da",
15      "instance-ids": [
16        "a648d98f-fdd8-4323-952a-a50a3e4e500f"
17      ],
18      "deployment-id": "606419dc-418e-489c-8531-bff9770fc346",
19      "command": "configure",
20      "status": "successful"
21    }
22 }
```

The duration field is only populated when a deployment is finished, and shows time in seconds.

AWS OpsWorks Stacks alert

An AWS OpsWorks Stacks service error was raised.

```
 1 {
 2    "version": "0",
 3    "id": "f99faa6f-0e27-e398-95bb-8f190806d275",
 4    "detail-type": "OpsWorks Alert",
 5    "source": "aws.opsworks",
 6    "account": "123456789012",
```

```
7      "time": "2018-01-20T16:51:29Z",
8      "region": "us-east-1",
9      "resources": [],
10     "detail": {
11       "stack-id": "2f48f2be-ac7d-4dd5-80bb-88375f94db7b",
12       "instance-id": "986efb74-69e8-4c6d-878e-5b77c054cbb0",
13       "type": "InstanceStop",
14       "message": "The shutdown of the instance timed out. Please try stopping it again."
15     }
16   }
```

AWS Systems Manager Events

The following are examples of the events for AWS Systems Manager. For more information, see Log Command Execution Status Changes for Run Command in the *Amazon EC2 User Guide for Linux Instances*.

Run Command Status-change Notification

```
1   {
2       "version": "0",
3       "id": "51c0891d-0e34-45b1-83d6-95db273d1602",
4       "detail-type": "EC2 Command Status-change Notification",
5       "source": "aws.ssm",
6       "account": "123456789012",
7       "time": "2016-07-10T21:51:32Z",
8       "region": "us-east-1",
9       "resources": ["arn:aws:ec2:us-east-1:123456789012:instance/i-abcd1111"],
10      "detail": {
11          "command-id": "e8d3c0e4-71f7-4491-898f-c9b35bee5f3b",
12          "document-name": "AWS-RunPowerShellScript",
13          "expire-after": "2016-07-14T22:01:30.049Z",
14          "parameters": {
15              "executionTimeout": ["3600"],
16              "commands": ["date"]
17          },
18          "requested-date-time": "2016-07-10T21:51:30.049Z",
19          "status": "Success"
20      }
21  }
```

Run Command Invocation Status-change Notification

```
1   {
2       "version": "0",
3       "id": "4780e1b8-f56b-4de5-95f2-95db273d1602",
4       "detail-type": "EC2 Command Invocation Status-change Notification",
5       "source": "aws.ssm",
6       "account": "123456789012",
7       "time": "2016-07-10T21:51:32Z",
8       "region": "us-east-1",
9       "resources": ["arn:aws:ec2:us-east-1:123456789012:instance/i-abcd1111"],
10      "detail": {
11          "command-id": "e8d3c0e4-71f7-4491-898f-c9b35bee5f3b",
12          "document-name": "AWS-RunPowerShellScript",
13          "instance-id": "i-9bb89e2b",
```

```
14        "requested-date-time": "2016-07-10T21:51:30.049Z",
15        "status": "Success"
16      }
17 }
```

Automation Step Status-change Notification

```
1  {
2    "version": "0",
3    "id": "eeca120b-a321-433e-9635-dab369006a6b",
4    "detail-type": "EC2 Automation Step Status-change Notification",
5    "source": "aws.ssm",
6    "account": "123456789012",
7    "time": "2016-11-29T19:43:35Z",
8    "region": "us-east-1",
9    "resources": ["arn:aws:ssm:us-east-1:123456789012:automation-execution/333ba70b-2333-48db-b17e
          -a5e69c6f4d1c",
10       "arn:aws:ssm:us-east-1:123456789012:automation-definition/runcommand1:1"],
11   "detail": {
12       "ExecutionId": "333ba70b-2333-48db-b17e-a5e69c6f4d1c",
13       "Definition": "runcommand1",
14       "DefinitionVersion": 1.0,
15       "Status": "Success",
16       "EndTime": "Nov 29, 2016 7:43:25 PM",
17       "StartTime": "Nov 29, 2016 7:43:23 PM",
18       "Time": 2630.0,
19       "StepName": "runFixedCmds",
20       "Action": "aws:runCommand"
21     }
22 }
```

Automation Execution Status-change Notification

```
1  {
2    "version": "0",
3    "id": "d290ece9-1088-4383-9df6-cd5b4ac42b99",
4    "detail-type": "EC2 Automation Execution Status-change Notification",
5    "source": "aws.ssm",
6    "account": "123456789012",
7    "time": "2016-11-29T19:43:35Z",
8    "region": "us-east-1",
9    "resources": ["arn:aws:ssm:us-east-1:123456789012:automation-execution/333ba70b-2333-48db-b17e
          -a5e69c6f4d1c",
10       "arn:aws:ssm:us-east-1:123456789012:automation-definition/runcommand1:1"],
11   "detail": {
12       "ExecutionId": "333ba70b-2333-48db-b17e-a5e69c6f4d1c",
13       "Definition": "runcommand1",
14       "DefinitionVersion": 1.0,
15       "Status": "Success",
16       "StartTime": "Nov 29, 2016 7:43:20 PM",
17       "EndTime": "Nov 29, 2016 7:43:26 PM",
18       "Time": 5753.0,
19       "ExecutedBy": "arn:aws:iam::123456789012:user/userName"
20     }
21 }
```

State Manager Association State Change

```
1  {
2      "version":"0",
3      "id":"db839caf-6f6c-40af-9a48-25b2ae2b7774",
4      "detail-type":"EC2 State Manager Association State Change",
5      "source":"aws.ssm",
6      "account":"123456789012",
7      "time":"2017-05-16T23:01:10Z",
8      "region":"us-west-1",
9      "resources":[
10         "arn:aws:ssm:us-west-1::document/AWS-RunPowerShellScript"
11     ],
12     "detail":{
13         "association-id":"6e37940a-23ba-4ab0-9b96-5d0a1a05464f",
14         "document-name":"AWS-RunPowerShellScript",
15         "association-version":"1",
16         "document-version":"Optional.empty",
17         "targets":"[{\"key\":\"InstanceIds\",\"values\":[\"i-12345678\"]}]",
18         "creation-date":"2017-02-13T17:22:54.458Z",
19         "last-successful-execution-date":"2017-05-16T23:00:01Z",
20         "last-execution-date":"2017-05-16T23:00:01Z",
21         "last-updated-date":"2017-02-13T17:22:54.458Z",
22         "status":"Success",
23         "association-status-aggregated-count":"{\"Success\":1}",
24         "schedule-expression":"cron(0 */30 * * * ? *)",
25         "association-cwe-version":"1.0"
26     }
27 }
```

State Manager Instance Association State Change

```
1  {
2      "version":"0",
3      "id":"6a7e8feb-b491-4cf7-a9f1-bf3703467718",
4      "detail-type":"EC2 State Manager Instance Association State Change",
5      "source":"aws.ssm",
6      "account":"123456789012",
7      "time":"2017-02-23T15:23:48Z",
8      "region":"us-east-1",
9      "resources":[
10         "arn:aws:ec2:us-east-1:123456789012:instance/i-12345678",
11         "arn:aws:ssm:us-east-1:123456789012:document/my-custom-document"
12     ],
13     "detail":{
14         "association-id":"34fcb7e0-9a14-4984-9989-0e04e3f60bd8",
15         "instance-id":"i-12345678",
16         "document-name":"my-custom-document",
17         "document-version":"1",
18         "targets":"[{\"key\":\"instanceids\",\"values\":[\"i-12345678\"]}]",
19         "creation-date":"2017-02-23T15:23:48Z",
20         "last-successful-execution-date":"2017-02-23T16:23:48Z",
21         "last-execution-date":"2017-02-23T16:23:48Z",
22         "status":"Success",
23         "detailed-status":"",
24         "error-code":"testErrorCode",
```

```
25        "execution-summary":"testExecutionSummary",
26        "output-url":"sampleurl",
27        "instance-association-cwe-version":"1"
28    }
29 }
```

AWS Systems Manager Parameter Store Events

The following are examples of the events for Amazon EC2 Systems Manager (SSM) Parameter Store.

Create Parameter

```
1  {
2    "version": "0",
3    "id": "6a7e4feb-b491-4cf7-a9f1-bf3703497718",
4    "detail-type": "Parameter Store Change",
5    "source": "aws.ssm",
6    "account": "123456789012",
7    "time": "2017-05-22T16:43:48Z",
8    "region": "us-east-1",
9    "resources": [
10     "arn:aws:ssm:us-east-1:123456789012:parameter/foo"
11   ],
12   "detail": {
13     "operation": "Create",
14     "name": "foo",
15     "type": "String",
16     "description": "Sample Parameter"
17   }
18 }
```

Update Parameter

```
1  {
2    "version": "0",
3    "id": "9547ef2d-3b7e-4057-b6cb-5fdf09ee7c8f",
4    "detail-type": "Parameter Store Change",
5    "source": "aws.ssm",
6    "account": "123456789012",
7    "time": "2017-05-22T16:44:48Z",
8    "region": "us-east-1",
9    "resources": [
10     "arn:aws:ssm:us-east-1:123456789012:parameter/foo"
11   ],
12   "detail": {
13     "operation": "Update",
14     "name": "foo",
15     "type": "String",
16     "description": "Sample Parameter"
17   }
18 }
```

Delete Parameter

```
1  {
```

```
2    "version": "0",
3    "id": "80e9b391-6a9b-413c-839a-453b528053af",
4    "detail-type": "Parameter Store Change",
5    "source": "aws.ssm",
6    "account": "123456789012",
7    "time": "2017-05-22T16:45:48Z",
8    "region": "us-east-1",
9    "resources": [
10     "arn:aws:ssm:us-east-1:123456789012:parameter/foo"
11   ],
12   "detail": {
13     "operation": "Delete",
14     "name": "foo",
15     "type": "String",
16     "description": "Sample Parameter"
17   }
18 }
```

AWS Systems Manager Configuration Compliance Events

The following are examples of the events for Amazon EC2 Systems Manager (SSM) configuration compliance.

Association Compliant

```
1  {
2    "version": "0",
3    "id": "01234567-0123-0123-0123-012345678901",
4    "detail-type": "Configuration Compliance State Change",
5    "source": "aws.ssm",
6    "account": "123456789012",
7    "time": "2017-07-17T19:03:26Z",
8    "region": "us-west-1",
9    "resources": [
10     "arn:aws:ssm:us-west-1:461348341421:managed-instance/i-01234567890abcdef"
11   ],
12   "detail": {
13     "last-runtime": "2017-01-01T10:10:10Z",
14     "compliance-status": "compliant",
15     "resource-type": "managed-instance",
16     "resource-id": "i-01234567890abcdef",
17     "compliance-type": "Association"
18   }
19 }
```

Association Non-Compliant

```
1  {
2    "version": "0",
3    "id": "01234567-0123-0123-0123-012345678901",
4    "detail-type": "Configuration Compliance State Change",
5    "source": "aws.ssm",
6    "account": "123456789012",
7    "time": "2017-07-17T19:02:31Z",
8    "region": "us-west-1",
9    "resources": [
```

```
10        "arn:aws:ssm:us-west-1:461348341421:managed-instance/i-01234567890abcdef"
11    ],
12    "detail": {
13      "last-runtime": "2017-01-01T10:10:10Z",
14      "compliance-status": "non_compliant",
15      "resource-type": "managed-instance",
16      "resource-id": "i-01234567890abcdef",
17      "compliance-type": "Association"
18    }
19  }
```

Patch Compliant

```
1  {
2    "version": "0",
3    "id": "01234567-0123-0123-0123-012345678901",
4    "detail-type": "Configuration Compliance State Change",
5    "source": "aws.ssm",
6    "account": "123456789012",
7    "time": "2017-07-17T19:03:26Z",
8    "region": "us-west-1",
9    "resources": [
10        "arn:aws:ssm:us-west-1:461348341421:managed-instance/i-01234567890abcdef"
11    ],
12    "detail": {
13      "resource-type": "managed-instance",
14      "resource-id": "i-01234567890abcdef",
15      "compliance-status": "compliant",
16      "compliance-type": "Patch",
17      "patch-baseline-id": "PB789",
18      "severity": "critical"
19    }
20  }
```

Patch Non-Compliant

```
1  {
2    "version": "0",
3    "id": "01234567-0123-0123-0123-012345678901",
4    "detail-type": "Configuration Compliance State Change",
5    "source": "aws.ssm",
6    "account": "123456789012",
7    "time": "2017-07-17T19:02:31Z",
8    "region": "us-west-1",
9    "resources": [
10        "arn:aws:ssm:us-west-1:461348341421:managed-instance/i-01234567890abcdef"
11    ],
12    "detail": {
13      "resource-type": "managed-instance",
14      "resource-id": "i-01234567890abcdef",
15      "compliance-status": "non_compliant",
16      "compliance-type": "Patch",
17      "patch-baseline-id": "PB789",
18      "severity": "critical"
19    }
20  }
```

Amazon EC2 Maintenance Windows Events

The following are examples of the events for Amazon EC2 Maintenance Windows.

Register a Target

The status could also be DEREGISTERED.

```
1  {
2      "version":"0",
3      "id":"01234567-0123-0123-0123-0123456789ab",
4      "detail-type":"Maintenance Window Target Registration Notification",
5      "source":"aws.ssm",
6      "account":"012345678901",
7      "time":"2016-11-16T00:58:37Z",
8      "region":"us-east-1",
9      "resources":[
10         "arn:aws:ssm:us-west-2:001312665065:maintenancewindow/mw-0ed7251d3fcf6e0c2",
11         "arn:aws:ssm:us-west-2:001312665065:windowtarget/e7265f13-3cc5-4f2f-97a9-7d3ca86c32a6"
12     ],
13     "detail":{
14         "window-target-id":"e7265f13-3cc5-4f2f-97a9-7d3ca86c32a6",
15         "window-id":"mw-0ed7251d3fcf6e0c2",
16         "status":"REGISTERED"
17     }
18 }
```

Window Execution Type

The other possibilities for status are PENDING, IN_PROGRESS, SUCCESS, FAILED, TIMED_OUT, and SKIPPED_OVERLAPPING.

```
1  {
2      "version":"0",
3      "id":"01234567-0123-0123-0123-0123456789ab",
4      "detail-type":"Maintenance Window Execution State-change Notification",
5      "source":"aws.ssm",
6      "account":"012345678901",
7      "time":"2016-11-16T01:00:57Z",
8      "region":"us-east-1",
9      "resources":[
10         "arn:aws:ssm:us-west-2:0123456789ab:maintenancewindow/mw-123456789012345678"
11     ],
12     "detail":{
13         "start-time":"2016-11-16T01:00:56.427Z",
14         "end-time":"2016-11-16T01:00:57.070Z",
15         "window-id":"mw-0ed7251d3fcf6e0c2",
16         "window-execution-id":"b60fb56e-776c-4e5c-84ee-123456789012",
17         "status":"TIMED_OUT"
18     }
19 }
```

Task Execution Type

The other possibilities for status are IN_PROGRESS, SUCCESS, FAILED, and TIMED_OUT.

```
1  {
2      "version":"0",
```

```
3      "id":"01234567-0123-0123-0123-0123456789ab",
4      "detail-type":"Maintenance Window Task Execution State-change Notification",
5      "source":"aws.ssm",
6      "account":"012345678901",
7      "time":"2016-11-16T01:00:56Z",
8      "region":"us-east-1",
9      "resources":[
10       "arn:aws:ssm:us-west-2:0123456789ab:maintenancewindow/mw-1234567890112345678"
11     ],
12     "detail":{
13       "start-time":"2016-11-16T01:00:56.759Z",
14       "task-execution-id":"6417e808-7f35-4d1a-843f-123456789012",
15       "end-time":"2016-11-16T01:00:56.847Z",
16       "window-id":"mw-0ed7251d3fcf6e0c2",
17       "window-execution-id":"b60fb56e-776c-4e5c-84ee-123456789012",
18       "status":"TIMED_OUT"
19     }
20   }
```

Task Target Processed

The other possibilities for status are IN_PROGRESS, SUCCESS, FAILED, and TIMED_OUT.

```
1    {
2      "version":"0",
3      "id":"01234567-0123-0123-0123-0123456789ab",
4      "detail-type":"Maintenance Window Task Target Invocation State-change Notification",
5      "source":"aws.ssm",
6      "account":"012345678901",
7      "time":"2016-11-16T01:00:57Z",
8      "region":"us-east-1",
9      "resources":[
10       "arn:aws:ssm:us-west-2:0123456789ab:maintenancewindow/mw-1234567890112345678"
11     ],
12     "detail":{
13       "start-time":"2016-11-16T01:00:56.427Z",
14       "end-time":"2016-11-16T01:00:57.070Z",
15       "window-id":"mw-0ed7251d3fcf6e0c2",
16       "window-execution-id":"b60fb56e-776c-4e5c-84ee-123456789012",
17       "task-execution-id":"6417e808-7f35-4d1a-843f-123456789012",
18       "window-target-id":"e7265f13-3cc5-4f2f-97a9-123456789012",
19       "status":"TIMED_OUT",
20       "owner-information":"Owner"
21     }
22   }
```

Window State Change

The possibilities for status are ENABLED and DISABLED.

```
1    {
2      "version":"0",
3      "id":"01234567-0123-0123-0123-0123456789ab",
4      "detail-type":"Maintenance Window State-change Notification",
5      "source":"aws.ssm",
6      "account":"012345678901",
7      "time":"2016-11-16T00:58:37Z",
```

```
 8      "region":"us-east-1",
 9      "resources":[
10         "arn:aws:ssm:us-west-2:0123456789ab:maintenancewindow/mw-123456789012345678"
11      ],
12      "detail":{
13         "window-id":"mw-123456789012",
14         "status":"DISABLED"
15      }
16   }
```

Amazon ECS Events

For Amazon ECS sample events, see Amazon ECS Events in the *Amazon Elastic Container Service Developer Guide*.

Amazon EMR Events

The following are examples of events for Amazon EMR.

Amazon EMR Auto Scaling Policy State Change

```
 1  {
 2      "version":"0",
 3      "id":"2f8147ab-8c48-47c6-b0b6-3ee23ec8d300",
 4      "detail-type":"EMR Auto Scaling Policy State Change",
 5      "source":"aws.emr",
 6      "account":"123456789012",
 7      "time":"2016-12-16T20:42:44Z",
 8      "region":"us-east-1",
 9      "resources":[],
10      "detail":{
11         "resourceId":"ig-X2LBMHTGPCBU",
12         "clusterId":"j-1YONHTCP3YZKC",
13         "state":"PENDING",
14         "message":"AutoScaling policy modified by user request",
15         "scalingResourceType":"INSTANCE_GROUP"
16      }
17   }
```

Amazon EMR Cluster State Change – Starting

```
 1  {
 2      "version": "0",
 3      "id": "999cccaa-eaaa-0000-1111-123456789012",
 4      "detail-type": "EMR Cluster State Change",
 5      "source": "aws.emr",
 6      "account": "123456789012",
 7      "time": "2016-12-16T20:43:05Z",
 8      "region": "us-east-1",
 9      "resources": [],
10      "detail": {
11         "severity": "INFO",
12         "stateChangeReason": "{\"code\":\"\"}",
13         "name": "Development Cluster",
```

```
14      "clusterId": "j-123456789ABCD",
15      "state": "STARTING",
16      "message": "Amazon EMR cluster j-123456789ABCD (Development Cluster) was requested at
            2016-12-16 20:42 UTC and  is being created."
17    }
18  }
```

Amazon EMR Cluster State Change – Terminated

```
1  {
2    "version": "0",
3    "id": "1234abb0-f87e-1234-b7b6-000000123456",
4    "detail-type": "EMR Cluster State Change",
5    "source": "aws.emr",
6    "account": "123456789012",
7    "time": "2016-12-16T21:00:23Z",
8    "region": "us-east-1",
9    "resources": [],
10   "detail": {
11     "severity": "INFO",
12     "stateChangeReason": "{\"code\":\"USER_REQUEST\",\"message\":\"Terminated by user request
            \"}",
13     "name": "Development Cluster",
14     "clusterId": "j-123456789ABCD",
15     "state": "TERMINATED",
16     "message": "Amazon EMR Cluster jj-123456789ABCD (Development Cluster) has terminated at
            2016-12-16 21:00 UTC with a reason of USER_REQUEST."
17   }
18 }
```

Amazon EMR Instance Group State Change

```
1  {
2    "version": "0",
3    "id": "999cccaa-eaaa-0000-1111-123456789012",
4    "detail-type": "EMR Instance Group State Change",
5    "source": "aws.emr",
6    "account": "123456789012",
7    "time": "2016-12-16T20:57:47Z",
8    "region": "us-east-1",
9    "resources": [],
10   "detail": {
11     "market": "ON_DEMAND",
12     "severity": "INFO",
13     "requestedInstanceCount": "2",
14     "instanceType": "m3.xlarge",
15     "instanceGroupType": "CORE",
16     "instanceGroupId": "ig-ABCDEFGHIJKL",
17     "clusterId": "j-123456789ABCD",
18     "runningInstanceCount": "2",
19     "state": "RUNNING",
20     "message": "The resizing operation for instance group ig-ABCDEFGHIJKL in Amazon EMR cluster
            j-123456789ABCD (Development Cluster) is complete. It now has an instance count of 2.
            The resize started at 2016-12-16 20:57 UTC and took 0 minutes to complete."
21   }
22 }
```

Amazon EMR Step Status Change

```
1  {
2    "version": "0",
3    "id": "999cccaa-eaaa-0000-1111-123456789012",
4    "detail-type": "EMR Step Status Change",
5    "source": "aws.emr",
6    "account": "123456789012",
7    "time": "2016-12-16T20:53:09Z",
8    "region": "us-east-1",
9    "resources": [],
10   "detail": {
11     "severity": "ERROR",
12     "actionOnFailure": "CONTINUE",
13     "stepId": "s-ZYXWVUTSRQPON",
14     "name": "CustomJAR",
15     "clusterId": "j-123456789ABCD",
16     "state": "FAILED",
17     "message": "Step s-ZYXWVUTSRQPON (CustomJAR) in Amazon EMR cluster j-123456789ABCD (
           Development Cluster) failed at 2016-12-16 20:53 UTC."
18   }
19 }
```

Amazon GameLift Event

The following are examples of Amazon GameLift events. For more information, see FlexMatch Events Reference in the *Amazon GameLift Developer Guide.*

Matchmaking Searching

```
1  {
2    "version": "0",
3    "id": "cc3d3ebe-1d90-48f8-b268-c96655b8f013",
4    "detail-type": "GameLift Matchmaking Event",
5    "source": "aws.gamelift",
6    "account": "123456789012",
7    "time": "2017-08-08T21:15:36.421Z",
8    "region": "us-west-2",
9    "resources": [
10     "arn:aws:gamelift:us-west-2:123456789012:matchmakingconfiguration/SampleConfiguration"
11   ],
12   "detail": {
13     "tickets": [
14       {
15         "ticketId": "ticket-1",
16         "startTime": "2017-08-08T21:15:35.676Z",
17         "players": [
18           {
19             "playerId": "player-1"
20           }
21         ]
22       }
23     ],
24     "estimatedWaitMillis": "NOT_AVAILABLE",
25     "type": "MatchmakingSearching",
```

```
26       "gameSessionInfo": {
27          "players": [
28             {
29                "playerId": "player-1"
30             }
31          ]
32       }
33    }
34 }
```

Potential Match Created

```
1  {
2     "version": "0",
3     "id": "fce8633f-aea3-45bc-aeba-99d639cad2d4",
4     "detail-type": "GameLift Matchmaking Event",
5     "source": "aws.gamelift",
6     "account": "123456789012",
7     "time": "2017-08-08T21:17:41.178Z",
8     "region": "us-west-2",
9     "resources": [
10       "arn:aws:gamelift:us-west-2:123456789012:matchmakingconfiguration/SampleConfiguration"
11    ],
12    "detail": {
13       "tickets": [
14          {
15             "ticketId": "ticket-1",
16             "startTime": "2017-08-08T21:15:35.676Z",
17             "players": [
18                {
19                   "playerId": "player-1",
20                   "team": "red"
21                }
22             ]
23          },
24          {
25             "ticketId": "ticket-2",
26             "startTime": "2017-08-08T21:17:40.657Z",
27             "players": [
28                {
29                   "playerId": "player-2",
30                   "team": "blue"
31                }
32             ]
33          }
34       ],
35       "acceptanceTimeout": 600,
36       "ruleEvaluationMetrics": [
37          {
38             "ruleName": "EvenSkill",
39             "passedCount": 3,
40             "failedCount": 0
41          },
42          {
43             "ruleName": "EvenTeams",
```

```json
44        "passedCount": 3,
45        "failedCount": 0
46      },
47      {
48        "ruleName": "FastConnection",
49        "passedCount": 3,
50        "failedCount": 0
51      },
52      {
53        "ruleName": "NoobSegregation",
54        "passedCount": 3,
55        "failedCount": 0
56      }
57    ],
58    "acceptanceRequired": true,
59    "type": "PotentialMatchCreated",
60    "gameSessionInfo": {
61      "players": [
62        {
63          "playerId": "player-1",
64          "team": "red"
65        },
66        {
67          "playerId": "player-2",
68          "team": "blue"
69        }
70      ]
71    },
72    "matchId": "3faf26ac-f06e-43e5-8d86-08feff26f692"
73  }
74 }
```

Accept Match

```json
1  {
2    "version": "0",
3    "id": "b3f76d66-c8e5-416a-aa4c-aa1278153edc",
4    "detail-type": "GameLift Matchmaking Event",
5    "source": "aws.gamelift",
6    "account": "123456789012",
7    "time": "2017-08-09T20:04:42.660Z",
8    "region": "us-west-2",
9    "resources": [
10      "arn:aws:gamelift:us-west-2:123456789012:matchmakingconfiguration/SampleConfiguration"
11    ],
12    "detail": {
13      "tickets": [
14        {
15          "ticketId": "ticket-1",
16          "startTime": "2017-08-09T20:01:35.305Z",
17          "players": [
18            {
19              "playerId": "player-1",
20              "team": "red"
21            }
```

```
22              ]
23          },
24          {
25              "ticketId": "ticket-2",
26              "startTime": "2017-08-09T20:04:16.637Z",
27              "players": [
28                  {
29                      "playerId": "player-2",
30                      "team": "blue",
31                      "accepted": false
32                  }
33              ]
34          }
35      ],
36      "type": "AcceptMatch",
37      "gameSessionInfo": {
38          "players": [
39              {
40                  "playerId": "player-1",
41                  "team": "red"
42              },
43              {
44                  "playerId": "player-2",
45                  "team": "blue",
46                  "accepted": false
47              }
48          ]
49      },
50      "matchId": "848b5f1f-0460-488e-8631-2960934d13e5"
51  }
52 }
```

Accept Match Completed

```
1  {
2      "version": "0",
3      "id": "b1990d3d-f737-4d6c-b150-af5ace8c35d3",
4      "detail-type": "GameLift Matchmaking Event",
5      "source": "aws.gamelift",
6      "account": "123456789012",
7      "time": "2017-08-08T20:43:14.621Z",
8      "region": "us-west-2",
9      "resources": [
10         "arn:aws:gamelift:us-west-2:123456789012:matchmakingconfiguration/SampleConfiguration"
11     ],
12     "detail": {
13         "tickets": [
14             {
15                 "ticketId": "ticket-1",
16                 "startTime": "2017-08-08T20:30:40.972Z",
17                 "players": [
18                     {
19                         "playerId": "player-1",
20                         "team": "red"
21                     }
```

```
22          ]
23        },
24        {
25          "ticketId": "ticket-2",
26          "startTime": "2017-08-08T20:33:14.111Z",
27          "players": [
28            {
29              "playerId": "player-2",
30              "team": "blue"
31            }
32          ]
33        }
34      ],
35      "acceptance": "TimedOut",
36      "type": "AcceptMatchCompleted",
37      "gameSessionInfo": {
38        "players": [
39          {
40            "playerId": "player-1",
41            "team": "red"
42          },
43          {
44            "playerId": "player-2",
45            "team": "blue"
46          }
47        ]
48      },
49      "matchId": "a0d9bd24-4695-4f12-876f-ea6386dd6dce"
50    }
51  }
```

Matchmaking Succeeded

```
1  {
2    "version": "0",
3    "id": "5ccb6523-0566-412d-b63c-1569e00d023d",
4    "detail-type": "GameLift Matchmaking Event",
5    "source": "aws.gamelift",
6    "account": "123456789012",
7    "time": "2017-08-09T19:59:09.159Z",
8    "region": "us-west-2",
9    "resources": [
10     "arn:aws:gamelift:us-west-2:123456789012:matchmakingconfiguration/SampleConfiguration"
11   ],
12   "detail": {
13     "tickets": [
14       {
15         "ticketId": "ticket-1",
16         "startTime": "2017-08-09T19:58:59.277Z",
17         "players": [
18           {
19             "playerId": "player-1",
20             "playerSessionId": "psess-6e7c13cf-10d6-4756-a53f-db7de782ed67",
21             "team": "red"
22           }
```

```
23            ]
24          },
25          {
26            "ticketId": "ticket-2",
27            "startTime": "2017-08-09T19:59:08.663Z",
28            "players": [
29              {
30                "playerId": "player-2",
31                "playerSessionId": "psess-786b342f-9c94-44eb-bb9e-c1de46c472ce",
32                "team": "blue"
33              }
34            ]
35          }
36        ],
37        "type": "MatchmakingSucceeded",
38        "gameSessionInfo": {
39          "gameSessionArn": "arn:aws:gamelift:us-west-2:123456789012:gamesession/836cf48d-bcb0-4a2c-
                  bec1-9c456541352a",
40          "ipAddress": "192.168.1.1",
41          "port": 10777,
42          "players": [
43            {
44              "playerId": "player-1",
45              "playerSessionId": "psess-6e7c13cf-10d6-4756-a53f-db7de782ed67",
46              "team": "red"
47            },
48            {
49              "playerId": "player-2",
50              "playerSessionId": "psess-786b342f-9c94-44eb-bb9e-c1de46c472ce",
51              "team": "blue"
52            }
53          ]
54        },
55        "matchId": "c0ec1a54-7fec-4b55-8583-76d67adb7754"
56      }
57 }
```

Matchmaking Timed Out

```
1  {
2    "version": "0",
3    "id": "fe528a7d-46ad-4bdc-96cb-b094b5f6bf56",
4    "detail-type": "GameLift Matchmaking Event",
5    "source": "aws.gamelift",
6    "account": "123456789012",
7    "time": "2017-08-09T20:11:35.598Z",
8    "region": "us-west-2",
9    "resources": [
10     "arn:aws:gamelift:us-west-2:123456789012:matchmakingconfiguration/SampleConfiguration"
11   ],
12   "detail": {
13     "reason": "TimedOut",
14     "tickets": [
15       {
16         "ticketId": "ticket-1",
```

```
17        "startTime": "2017-08-09T20:01:35.305Z",
18        "players": [
19          {
20            "playerId": "player-1",
21            "team": "red"
22          }
23        ]
24      }
25    ],
26    "ruleEvaluationMetrics": [
27      {
28        "ruleName": "EvenSkill",
29        "passedCount": 3,
30        "failedCount": 0
31      },
32      {
33        "ruleName": "EvenTeams",
34        "passedCount": 3,
35        "failedCount": 0
36      },
37      {
38        "ruleName": "FastConnection",
39        "passedCount": 3,
40        "failedCount": 0
41      },
42      {
43        "ruleName": "NoobSegregation",
44        "passedCount": 3,
45        "failedCount": 0
46      }
47    ],
48    "type": "MatchmakingTimedOut",
49    "message": "Removed from matchmaking due to timing out.",
50    "gameSessionInfo": {
51      "players": [
52        {
53          "playerId": "player-1",
54          "team": "red"
55        }
56      ]
57    }
58  }
59 }
```

Matchmaking Cancelled

```
1 {
2   "version": "0",
3   "id": "8d6f84da-5e15-4741-8d5c-5ac99091c27f",
4   "detail-type": "GameLift Matchmaking Event",
5   "source": "aws.gamelift",
6   "account": "123456789012",
7   "time": "2017-08-09T20:00:07.843Z",
8   "region": "us-west-2",
9   "resources": [
```

```
10        "arn:aws:gamelift:us-west-2:123456789012:matchmakingconfiguration/SampleConfiguration"
11      ],
12      "detail": {
13        "reason": "Cancelled",
14        "tickets": [
15          {
16            "ticketId": "ticket-1",
17            "startTime": "2017-08-09T19:59:26.118Z",
18            "players": [
19              {
20                "playerId": "player-1"
21              }
22            ]
23          }
24        ],
25        "ruleEvaluationMetrics": [
26          {
27            "ruleName": "EvenSkill",
28            "passedCount": 0,
29            "failedCount": 0
30          },
31          {
32            "ruleName": "EvenTeams",
33            "passedCount": 0,
34            "failedCount": 0
35          },
36          {
37            "ruleName": "FastConnection",
38            "passedCount": 0,
39            "failedCount": 0
40          },
41          {
42            "ruleName": "NoobSegregation",
43            "passedCount": 0,
44            "failedCount": 0
45          }
46        ],
47        "type": "MatchmakingCancelled",
48        "message": "Cancelled by request.",
49        "gameSessionInfo": {
50          "players": [
51            {
52              "playerId": "player-1"
53            }
54          ]
55        }
56      }
57    }
```

Matchmaking Failed

```
1  {
2    "version": "0",
3    "id": "025b55a4-41ac-4cf4-89d1-f2b3c6fd8f9d",
4    "detail-type": "GameLift Matchmaking Event",
```

```
 5     "source": "aws.gamelift",
 6     "account": "123456789012",
 7     "time": "2017-08-16T18:41:09.970Z",
 8     "region": "us-west-2",
 9     "resources": [
10       "arn:aws:gamelift:us-west-2:123456789012:matchmakingconfiguration/SampleConfiguration"
11     ],
12     "detail": {
13       "tickets": [
14         {
15           "ticketId": "ticket-1",
16           "startTime": "2017-08-16T18:41:02.631Z",
17           "players": [
18             {
19               "playerId": "player-1",
20               "team": "red"
21             }
22           ]
23         }
24       ],
25       "customEventData": "foo",
26       "type": "MatchmakingFailed",
27       "reason": "UNEXPECTED_ERROR",
28       "message": "An unexpected error was encountered during match placing.",
29       "gameSessionInfo": {
30         "players": [
31           {
32             "playerId": "player-1",
33             "team": "red"
34           }
35         ]
36       },
37       "matchId": "3ea83c13-218b-43a3-936e-135cc570cba7"
38     }
39 }
```

AWS Glue Events

The following is the format for AWS Glue events.

Successful Job Run

```
 1 {
 2     "version":"0",
 3     "id":"abcdef00-1234-5678-9abc-def012345678",
 4     "detail-type":"Glue Job State Change",
 5     "source":"aws.glue",
 6     "account":"123456789012",
 7     "time":"2017-09-07T18:57:21Z",
 8     "region":"us-west-2",
 9     "resources":[],
10     "detail":{
11         "jobName":"MyJob",
12         "severity":"INFO",
```

```
13        "state":"SUCCEEDED",
14        "jobRunId":"jr_abcdef0123456789abcdef0123456789abcdef0123456789abcdef0123456789",
15        "message":"Job run succeeded"
16    }
17 }
```

Failed Job Run

```
1 {
2     "version":"0",
3     "id":"abcdef01-1234-5678-9abc-def012345678",
4     "detail-type":"Glue Job State Change",
5     "source":"aws.glue",
6     "account":"123456789012",
7     "time":"2017-09-07T06:02:03Z",
8     "region":"us-west-2",
9     "resources":[],
10    "detail":{
11        "jobName":"MyJob",
12        "severity":"ERROR",
13        "state":"FAILED",
14        "jobRunId":"jr_0123456789abcdef0123456789abcdef0123456789abcdef0123456789abcdef",
15        "message":"JobName:MyJob and JobRunId:
               jr_0123456789abcdef0123456789abcdef0123456789abcdef0123456789abcdef failed to
               execute with exception Role arn:aws:iam::123456789012:role/Glue_Role should be given
               assume role permissions for Glue Service."
16    }
17 }
```

Stopped Job Run

```
1 {
2 "version":"0",
3 "id":"abcdef00-1234-5678-9abc-def012345678",
4 "detail-type":"Glue Job State Change",
5 "source":"aws.glue",
6 "account":"123456789012",
7 "time":"2017-11-20T20:22:06Z",
8 "region":"us-east-1",
9 "resources":[],
10 "detail":{
11 "jobName":"MyJob",
12 "severity":"INFO",
13 "state":"STOPPED",
14 "jobRunId":"jr_abc0123456789abcdef0123456789abcdef0123456789abcdef0123456789def",
15 "message":"Job run stopped"
16 }
17 }
```

Crawler Started

```
1 {
2     "version":"0",
3     "id":"05efe8a2-c309-6884-a41b-3508bcdc9695",
4     "detail-type":"Glue Crawler State Change",
5     "source":"aws.glue",
```

```
 6    "account":"561226563745",
 7    "time":"2017-11-11T01:09:46Z",
 8    "region":"us-east-1",
 9    "resources":[
10
11    ],
12    "detail":{
13       "accountId":"561226563745",
14       "crawlerName":"S3toS3AcceptanceTestCrawlera470bd94-9e00-4518-8942-e80c8431c322",
15       "startTime":"2017-11-11T01:09:46Z",
16       "state":"Started",
17       "message":"Crawler Started"
18    }
19 }
```

Crawler Succeeded

```
 1 {
 2    "version":"0",
 3    "id":"3d675db5-59b9-6388-b8e8-e0a9b6d567a9",
 4    "detail-type":"Glue Crawler State Change",
 5    "source":"aws.glue",
 6    "account":"561226563745",
 7    "time":"2017-11-11T01:25:00Z",
 8    "region":"us-east-1",
 9    "resources":[
10
11    ],
12    "detail":{
13       "tablesCreated":"0",
14       "warningMessage":"N/A",
15       "partitionsUpdated":"0",
16       "tablesUpdated":"0",
17       "message":"Crawler Succeeded",
18       "partitionsDeleted":"0",
19       "accountId":"561226563745",
20       "runningTime (sec)":"7",
21       "tablesDeleted":"0",
22       "crawlerName":"SchedulerTestCrawler51fb3a8b-1015-49f0-a969-ca126680b94b",
23       "completionDate":"2017-11-11T01:25:00Z",
24       "state":"Succeeded",
25       "partitionsCreated":"0",
26       "cloudWatchLogLink":"https://console.aws.amazon.com/cloudwatch/home?region=us-east-1#
             logEventViewer:group=/aws-glue/crawlers;stream=SchedulerTestCrawler51fb3a8b-1015-49f0-
             a969-ca126680b94b"
27    }
28 }
```

Crawler Failed

```
 1 {
 2    "version":"0",
 3    "id":"f7965b59-470f-2e06-bb89-a8cebaabefac",
 4    "detail-type":"Glue Crawler State Change",
 5    "source":"aws.glue",
 6    "account":"782104008917",
```

```
7      "time":"2017-10-20T05:10:08Z",
8      "region":"us-east-1",
9      "resources":[
10
11     ],
12     "detail":{
13        "crawlerName":"test-crawler-notification",
14        "errorMessage":"Internal Service Exception",
15        "accountId":"1234",
16        "cloudWatchLogLink":"https://console.aws.amazon.com/cloudwatch/home?region=us-east-1#
                logEventViewer:group=/aws-glue/crawlers;stream=test-crawler-notification",
17        "state":"Failed",
18        "message":"Crawler Failed"
19     }
20 }
```

Amazon GuardDuty Events

For information about example Amazon GuardDuty events, see Monitoring Amazon GuardDuty with Amazon CloudWatch Events in the *Amazon GuardDuty User Guide*.

AWS Health Events

The following is the format for the AWS Personal Health Dashboard (AWS Health) events. For more information, see Managing AWS Health Events with Amazon CloudWatch Events in the *AWS Health User Guide*.

AWS Health Event Format

```
1  {
2    "version": "0",
3    "id": "7bf73129-1428-4cd3-a780-95db273d1602",
4    "detail-type": "AWS Health Event",
5    "source": "aws.health",
6    "account": "123456789012",
7    "time": "2016-06-05T06:27:57Z",
8    "region": "region",
9    "resources": [],
10   "detail": {
11     "eventArn": "arn:aws:health:region::event/id",
12     "service": "service",
13     "eventTypeCode": "AWS_service_code",
14     "eventTypeCategory": "category",
15     "startTime": "Sun, 05 Jun 2016 05:01:10 GMT",
16     "endTime": "Sun, 05 Jun 2016 05:30:57 GMT",
17     "eventDescription": [{
18       "language": "lang-code",
19       "latestDescription": "description"
20     }]
21     ...
22   }
23 }
```

eventTypeCategory
The category code of the event. The possible values are `issue`, `accountNotification`, and `scheduledChange`.

eventTypeCode

The unique identifier for the event type. Examples include `AWS_EC2_INSTANCE_NETWORK_MAINTENANCE_SCHEDULED` and `AWS_EC2_INSTANCE_REBOOT_MAINTENANCE_SCHEDULED`. Events that include `MAINTENANCE_SCHEDULED` are usually pushed out about two weeks before the `startTime`.

id

The unique identifier for the event.

service

The AWS service affected by the event. For example, `EC2`, `S3`, `REDSHIFT`, or `RDS`.

Elastic Load Balancing API Issue

```
{
  "version": "0",
  "id": "121345678-1234-1234-1234-123456789012",
  "detail-type": "AWS Health Event",
  "source": "aws.health",
  "account": "123456789012",
  "time": "2016-06-05T06:27:57Z",
  "region": "ap-southeast-2",
  "resources": [],
  "detail": {
    "eventArn": "arn:aws:health:ap-southeast-2::event/
        AWS_ELASTICLOADBALANCING_API_ISSUE_90353408594353980",
    "service": "ELASTICLOADBALANCING",
    "eventTypeCode": "AWS_ELASTICLOADBALANCING_API_ISSUE",
    "eventTypeCategory": "issue",
    "startTime": "Sat, 11 Jun 2016 05:01:10 GMT",
    "endTime": "Sat, 11 Jun 2016 05:30:57 GMT",
    "eventDescription": [{
      "language": "en_US",
      "latestDescription": "A description of the event will be provided here"
    }
  }
}
```

Amazon EC2 Instance Store Drive Performance Degraded

```
{
  "version": "0",
  "id": "121345678-1234-1234-1234-123456789012",
  "detail-type": "AWS Health Event",
  "source": "aws.health",
  "account": "123456789012",
  "time": "2016-06-05T06:27:57Z",
  "region": "us-west-2",
  "resources": [
    "i-abcd1111"
  ],
  "detail": {
    "eventArn": "arn:aws:health:us-west-2::event/
        AWS_EC2_INSTANCE_STORE_DRIVE_PERFORMANCE_DEGRADED_90353408594353980",
    "service": "EC2",
    "eventTypeCode": "AWS_EC2_INSTANCE_STORE_DRIVE_PERFORMANCE_DEGRADED",
    "eventTypeCategory": "issue",
    "startTime": "Sat, 05 Jun 2016 15:10:09 GMT",
    "eventDescription": [{
```

```
19    "language": "en_US",
20    "latestDescription": "A description of the event will be provided here"
21  }],
22  "affectedEntities": [{
23    "entityValue": "i-abcd1111",
24    "tags": {
25      "stage": "prod",
26      "app": "my-app"
27  }
28 }
```

AWS KMS Events

The following are examples of the AWS Key Management Service (AWS KMS) events. For more information, see AWS KMS Events in the *AWS Key Management Service Developer Guide.*

KMS CMK Rotation

AWS KMS automatically rotated a CMK's key material.

```
1 {
2    "version": "0",
3    "id": "6a7e8feb-b491-4cf7-a9f1-bf3703467718",
4    "detail-type": "KMS CMK Rotation",
5    "source": "aws.kms",
6    "account": "111122223333",
7    "time": "2016-08-25T21:05:33Z",
8    "region": "us-west-2",
9    "resources": [
10     "arn:aws:kms:us-west-2:111122223333:key/1234abcd-12ab-34cd-56ef-1234567890ab"
11   ],
12   "detail": {
13     "key-id": "1234abcd-12ab-34cd-56ef-1234567890ab"
14   }
15 }
```

KMS Imported Key Material Expiration

AWS KMS deleted a CMK's expired key material.

```
1 {
2    "version": "0",
3    "id": "9da9af57-9253-4406-87cb-7cc400e43465",
4    "detail-type": "KMS Imported Key Material Expiration",
5    "source": "aws.kms",
6    "account": "111122223333",
7    "time": "2016-08-22T20:12:19Z",
8    "region": "us-west-2",
9    "resources": [
10     "arn:aws:kms:us-west-2:111122223333:key/1234abcd-12ab-34cd-56ef-1234567890ab"
11   ],
12   "detail": {
13     "key-id": "1234abcd-12ab-34cd-56ef-1234567890ab"
14   }
15 }
```

KMS CMK Deletion

AWS KMS completed a scheduled CMK deletion.

```
1  {
2    "version": "0",
3    "id": "e9ce3425-7d22-412a-a699-e7a5fc3fbc9a",
4    "detail-type": "KMS CMK Deletion",
5    "source": "aws.kms",
6    "account": "111122223333",
7    "time": "2016-08-19T03:23:45Z",
8    "region": "us-west-2",
9    "resources": [
10     "arn:aws:kms:us-west-2:111122223333:key/1234abcd-12ab-34cd-56ef-1234567890ab"
11   ],
12   "detail": {
13     "key-id": "1234abcd-12ab-34cd-56ef-1234567890ab"
14   }
15 }
```

Amazon Macie Events

The following are examples of Amazon Macie events.

Alert Created

```
1  {
2    "version": "0",
3    "id": "CWE-event-id",
4    "detail-type": "Macie Alert",
5    "source": "aws.macie",
6    "account": "123456789012",
7    "time": "2017-04-24T22:28:49Z",
8    "region": "us-east-1",
9    "resources": [
10     "arn:aws:macie:us-east-1:123456789012:trigger/trigger_id/alert/alert_id",
11     "arn:aws:macie:us-east-1:123456789012:trigger/trigger_id"
12   ],
13   "detail": {
14     "notification-type": "ALERT_CREATED",
15     "name": "Scanning bucket policies",
16     "tags": [
17       "Custom_Alert",
18       "Insider"
19     ],
20     "url": "https://lb00.us-east-1.macie.aws.amazon.com/111122223333/posts/alert_id",
21     "alert-arn": "arn:aws:macie:us-east-1:123456789012:trigger/trigger_id/alert/alert_id",
22     "risk-score": 80,
23     "trigger": {
24       "rule-arn": "arn:aws:macie:us-east-1:123456789012:trigger/trigger_id",
25       "alert-type": "basic",
26       "created-at": "2017-01-02 19:54:00.644000",
27       "description": "Alerting on failed enumeration of large number of bucket policies",
28       "risk": 8
29     },
```

```json
30      "created-at": "2017-04-18T00:21:12.059000",
31      "actor": "555566667777:assumed-role:superawesome:aroaidpldc7nsesfnheji",
32      "summary": {
33        "Description": "Alerting on failed enumeration of large number of bucket policies",
34        "IP": {
35          "34.199.185.34": 121,
36          "34.205.153.2": 2,
37          "72.21.196.70": 2
38        },
39        "Time Range": [
40          {
41            "count": 125,
42            "start": "2017-04-24T20:23:49Z",
43            "end": "2017-04-24T20:25:54Z"
44          }
45        ],
46        "Source ARN": "arn:aws:sts::123456789012:assumed-role/RoleName",
47        "Record Count": 1,
48        "Location": {
49          "us-east-1": 125
50        },
51        "Event Count": 125,
52        "Events": {
53          "GetBucketLocation": {
54            "count": 48,
55            "ISP": {
56              "Amazon": 48
57            }
58          },
59          "ListRoles": {
60            "count": 2,
61            "ISP": {
62              "Amazon": 2
63            }
64          },
65          "GetBucketPolicy": {
66            "count": 37,
67            "ISP": {
68              "Amazon": 37
69            },
70            "Error Code": {
71              "NoSuchBucketPolicy": 22
72            }
73          },
74          "GetBucketAcl": {
75            "count": 37,
76            "ISP": {
77              "Amazon": 37
78            }
79          },
80          "ListBuckets": {
81            "count": 1,
82            "ISP": {
83              "Amazon": 1
```

```
84            }
85          }
86        },
87        "recipientAccountId": {
88          "123456789012": 125
89        }
90      }
91    }
92 }


 1 {
 2   "version": "0",
 3   "id": "CWE-event-id",
 4   "detail-type": "Macie Alert",
 5   "source": "aws.macie",
 6   "account": "123456789012",
 7   "time": "2017-04-18T18:15:41Z",
 8   "region": "us-east-1",
 9   "resources": [
10     "arn:aws:macie:us-east-1:123456789012:trigger/trigger_id/alert/alert_id",
11     "arn:aws:macie:us-east-1:123456789012:trigger/trigger_id"
12   ],
13   "detail": {
14     "notification-type": "ALERT_CREATED",
15     "name": "Bucket is writable by all authenticated users",
16     "tags": [
17       "Custom_Alert",
18       "Audit"
19     ],
20     "url": "https://1b00.us-east-1.macie.aws.amazon.com/111122223333/posts/alert_id",
21     "alert-arn": "arn:aws:macie:us-east-1:123456789012:trigger/trigger_id/alert/alert_id",
22     "risk-score": 70,
23     "trigger": {
24       "rule-arn": "arn:aws:macie:us-east-1:123456789012:trigger/trigger_id",
25       "alert-type": "basic",
26       "created-at": "2017-04-08 00:21:30.749000",
27       "description": "Bucket is writable by all authenticated users",
28       "risk": 7
29     },
30     "created-at": "2017-04-18T18:16:17.046454",
31     "actor": "444455556666",
32     "summary": {
33       "Description": "Bucket is writable by all authenticated users",
34       "Bucket": {
35         "secret-bucket-name": 1
36       },
37       "Record Count": 1,
38       "ACL": {
39         "secret-bucket-name": [
40           {
41             "Owner": {
42               "DisplayName": "bucket_owner",
43               "ID": "089d2842f4b392f5c5c61f073bd2e4a37b3bb2e62659318c6960e8981648a17e"
44             },
45             "Grants": [
```

```
46              {
47                "Grantee": {
48                  "Type": "Group",
49                  "URI": "http://acs.amazonaws.com/groups/global/AuthenticatedUsers"
50                },
51                "Permission": "WRITE"
52              }
53            ]
54          }
55        ]
56      },
57      "Event Count": 1,
58      "Timestamps": {
59        "2017-01-10T22:48:06.784937": 1
60      }
61    }
62  }
63 }
```

Alert Updated

```
1  {
2    "version": "0",
3    "id": "CWE-event-id",
4    "detail-type": "Macie Alert",
5    "source": "aws.macie",
6    "account": "123456789012",
7    "time": "2017-04-18T17:47:48Z",
8    "region": "us-east-1",
9    "resources": [
10     "arn:aws:macie:us-east-1:123456789012:trigger/trigger_id/alert/alert_id",
11     "arn:aws:macie:us-east-1:123456789012:trigger/trigger_id"
12   ],
13   "detail": {
14     "notification-type": "ALERT_UPDATED",
15     "name": "Public bucket contains high risk object",
16     "tags": [
17       "Custom_Alert",
18       "Audit"
19     ],
20     "url": "https://lb00.us-east-1.macie.aws.amazon.com/111122223333/posts/alert_id",
21     "alert-arn": "arn:aws:macie:us-east-1:123456789012:trigger/trigger_id/alert/alert_id",
22     "risk-score": 100,
23     "trigger": {
24       "rule-arn": "arn:aws:macie:us-east-1:123456789012:trigger/trigger_id",
25       "alert-type": "basic",
26       "created-at": "2017-04-08 00:23:39.138000",
27       "description": "Public bucket contains high risk object",
28       "risk": 10
29     },
30     "created-at": "2017-04-08T00:36:26.270000",
31     "actor": "public_bucket",
32     "summary": {
33       "Description": "Public bucket contains high risk object",
34       "Object": {
```

```
35        "public_bucket/secret_key.txt": 1,
36        "public_bucket/financial_summary.txt": 1
37      },
38      "Record Count": 2,
39      "Themes": {
40        "Secret Markings": 1,
41        "Corporate Proposals": 1,
42        "Confidential Markings": 1
43      },
44      "Event Count": 2,
45      "DLP risk": {
46        "7": 2
47      },
48      "Owner": {
49        "bucket_owner": 2
50      },
51      "Timestamps": {
52        "2017-04-03T16:12:53+00:00": 2
53      }
54    }
55  }
56 }


1  {
2    "version": "0",
3    "id": "CWE-event-id",
4    "detail-type": "Macie Alert",
5    "source": "aws.macie",
6    "account": "123456789012",
7    "time": "2017-04-22T03:31:47Z",
8    "region": "us-east-1",
9    "resources": [
10     "arn:aws:macie:us-east-1:123456789012:trigger/macie/alert/alert_id",
11     "arn:aws:macie:us-east-1:123456789012:trigger/macie"
12   ],
13   "detail": {
14     "notification-type": "ALERT_UPDATED",
15     "name": "Lists the instance profiles that have the specified associated IAM role, Lists the
             names of the inline policies that are embedded in the specified IAM role",
16     "tags": [
17       "Predictive",
18       "Behavioral_Anomaly"
19     ],
20     "url": "https://lb00.us-east-1.macie.aws.amazon.com/111122223333/posts/alert_id",
21     "alert-arn": "arn:aws:macie:us-east-1:123456789012:trigger/macie/alert/alert_id",
22     "risk-score": 20,
23     "created-at": "2017-04-22T03:08:35.256000",
24     "actor": "123456789012:assumed-role:rolename",
25     "trigger": {
26       "alert-type": "predictive",
27       "features": {
28         "distinctEventName": {
29           "name": "distinctEventName",
30           "description": "Event Names executed during a user session",
31           "narrative": "A sudden increase in event names utilized by a user can be an indicator
```

```
                    of a change in user behavior or account risk",
32                  "risk": 3
33              },
34              "ListInstanceProfilesForRole": {
35                  "name": "ListInstanceProfilesForRole",
36                  "description": "Lists the instance profiles that have the specified associated IAM
                        role",
37                  "narrative": "Information collection activity suggesting the start of a reconnaissance
                        or exfiltration campaign",
38                  "anomalous": true,
39                  "multiplier": 8.420560747663552,
40                  "excession_times": [
41                      "2017-04-21T18:00:00Z"
42                  ],
43                  "risk": 1
44              },
45              "ListRolePolicies": {
46                  "name": "ListRolePolicies",
47                  "description": "Lists the names of the inline policies that are embedded in the
                        specified IAM role",
48                  "narrative": "Information collection activity suggesting the start of a reconnaisance
                        or exfiltration campaign",
49                  "anomalous": true,
50                  "multiplier": 12.017441860465116,
51                  "excession_times": [
52                      "2017-04-21T18:00:00Z"
53                  ],
54                  "risk": 2
55              }
56          }
57      }
58  }
59 }
```

Scheduled Events

The following is an example of a scheduled event:

```
1  {
2    "id": "53dc4d37-cffa-4f76-80c9-8b7d4a4d2eaa",
3    "detail-type": "Scheduled Event",
4    "source": "aws.events",
5    "account": "123456789012",
6    "time": "2015-10-08T16:53:06Z",
7    "region": "us-east-1",
8    "resources": [ "arn:aws:events:us-east-1:123456789012:rule/MyScheduledRule" ],
9    "detail": {}
10 }
```

AWS Server Migration Service Events

The following are examples of the events for AWS Server Migration Service.

Deleted replication job notification

```
1  {
2      "version": "0",
3      "id": "5630992d-92cd-439f-f2a8-92c8212aee24",
4      "detail-type": "Server Migration Job State Change",
5      "source": "aws.sms",
6      "account": "123456789012",
7      "time": "2018-02-07T22:30:11Z",
8      "region": "us-west-1",
9      "resources": [
10         "arn:aws:sms:us-west-1:123456789012:sms-job-21a64348"
11     ],
12     "detail": {
13         "state": "Deleted",
14         "replication-run-id": "N/A",
15         "replication-job-id": "sms-job-21a64348",
16         "version": "1.0"
17     }
18 }
```

Completed replication job notification

```
1  {
2      "version": "0",
3      "id": "3f9c59cc-f941-522a-be6d-f08e44ff1715",
4      "detail-type": "Server Migration Job State Change",
5      "source": "aws.sms",
6      "account": "123456789012",
7      "time": "2018-02-07T22:54:00Z",
8      "region": "us-west-1",
9      "resources": [
10         "arn:aws:sms:us-west-1:123456789012:sms-job-2ea64347",
11         "arn:aws:sms:us-west-1:123456789012:sms-job-2ea64347/sms-run-e1a64388"
12     ],
13     "detail": {
14         "state": "Completed",
15         "replication-run-id": "sms-run-e1a64388",
16         "replication-job-id": "sms-job-2ea64347",
17         "ami-id": "ami-746d6314",
18         "version": "1.0"
19     }
20 }
```

AWS Trusted Advisor Events

The following are examples of the events for AWS Trusted Advisor. For more information, see Monitoring Trusted Advisor Check Results with Amazon CloudWatch Events in the *AWS Support User Guide*.

Low Utilization Amazon EC2 Instances

```
1  {
2    "version": "0",
3    "id": "1234abcd-ab12-123a-123a-1234567890ab",
4    "detail-type": "Trusted Advisor Check Item Refresh Notification",
```

```
 5    "source": "aws.trustedadvisor",
 6    "account": "123456789012",
 7    "time": "2018-01-12T20:07:49Z",
 8    "region": "us-east-2",
 9    "resources": [],
10    "detail": {
11      "check-name": "Low Utilization Amazon EC2 Instances",
12      "check-item-detail": {
13        "Day 1": "0.1%  0.00MB",
14        "Day 2": "0.1%  0.00MB",
15        "Day 3": "0.1%  0.00MB",
16        "Region/AZ": "ca-central-1a",
17        "Estimated Monthly Savings": "$9.22",
18        "14-Day Average CPU Utilization": "0.1%",
19        "Day 14": "0.1%  0.00MB",
20        "Day 13": "0.1%  0.00MB",
21        "Day 12": "0.1%  0.00MB",
22        "Day 11": "0.1%  0.00MB",
23        "Day 10": "0.1%  0.00MB",
24        "14-Day Average Network I/O": "0.00MB",
25        "Number of Days Low Utilization": "14 days",
26        "Instance Type": "t2.micro",
27        "Instance ID": "i-01234567890abcdef",
28        "Day 8": "0.1%  0.00MB",
29        "Instance Name": null,
30        "Day 9": "0.1%  0.00MB",
31        "Day 4": "0.1%  0.00MB",
32        "Day 5": "0.1%  0.00MB",
33        "Day 6": "0.1%  0.00MB",
34        "Day 7": "0.1%  0.00MB"
35      },
36      "status": "WARN",
37      "resource_id": "arn:aws:ec2:ca-central-1:123456789012:instance/i-01234567890abcdef",
38      "uuid": "aa12345f-55c7-498e-b7ac-123456789012"
39    }
40 }
```

Load Balancer Optimization

```
 1 {
 2    "version": "0",
 3    "id": "1234abcd-ab12-123a-123a-1234567890ab",
 4    "detail-type": "Trusted Advisor Check Item Refresh Notification",
 5    "source": "aws.trustedadvisor",
 6    "account": "123456789012",
 7    "time": "2018-01-12T20:07:03Z",
 8    "region": "us-east-2",
 9    "resources": [],
10    "detail": {
11      "check-name": "Load Balancer Optimization ",
12      "check-item-detail": {
13        "Instances in Zone a": "1",
14        "Status": "Yellow",
15        "Instances in Zone b": "0",
16        "# of Zones": "2",
```

```
17        "Region": "eu-central-1",
18        "Load Balancer Name": "my-load-balance",
19        "Instances in Zone e": null,
20        "Instances in Zone c": null,
21        "Reason": "Single AZ",
22        "Instances in Zone d": null
23      },
24      "status": "WARN",
25      "resource_id": "arn:aws:elasticloadbalancing:eu-central-1:123456789012:loadbalancer/my-load-
            balancer",
26      "uuid": "aa12345f-55c7-498e-b7ac-123456789012"
27    }
28  }
```

Exposed Access Keys

```
1  {
2    "version": "0",
3    "id": "1234abcd-ab12-123a-123a-1234567890ab",
4    "detail-type": "Trusted Advisor Check Item Refresh Notification",
5    "source": "aws.trustedadvisor",
6    "account": "123456789012",
7    "time": "2018-01-12T19:38:24Z",
8    "region": "us-east-1",
9    "resources": [],
10   "detail": {
11     "check-name": "Exposed Access Keys",
12     "check-item-detail": {
13       "Case ID": "12345678-1234-1234-abcd-1234567890ab",
14       "Usage (USD per Day)": "0",
15       "User Name (IAM or Root)": "my-username",
16       "Deadline": "1440453299248",
17       "Access Key ID": "AKIAIOSFODNN7EXAMPLE",
18       "Time Updated": "1440021299248",
19       "Fraud Type": "Exposed",
20       "Location": "www.example.com"
21     },
22     "status": "ERROR",
23     "resource_id": "",
24     "uuid": "aa12345f-55c7-498e-b7ac-123456789012"
25   }
26 }
```

Sending and Receiving Events Between AWS Accounts

You can set up your AWS account to send events to another AWS account, or to receive events from another account. This can be useful if the two accounts belong to the same organization, or belong to organizations that are partners or have a similar relationship.

If you set up your account to send or receive events, you can specify which AWS accounts it sends events to or receives events from.

The overall process is as follows:

- Edit the *receiver* account permissions on its default *event bus* to allow one or more specified accounts (or all AWS accounts) to send events to the receiver account.
- On the *sender* account, set up one or more rules that have the receiver account's default event bus as the target.
- On the *receiver* account, set up one or more rules that match events that come from the sender account.

The AWS Region where the receiver account adds permissions to the default event bus must be the same region where the sender account creates the rule to send events to the receiver account.

Events sent from one account to another are charged to the sending account as custom events. The receiving account is not charged. For more information about CloudWatch Events pricing, see Amazon CloudWatch Pricing.

A receiver account can set up a rule that sends events received from a sender account on to a third account, however these events are not sent to the third account.

Enabling Your AWS Account to Receive Events from Other AWS Accounts

To receive events from other accounts, you must first edit the permissions on your account's default *event bus*. The default event bus accepts events from AWS services, other authorized AWS accounts, and `PutEvents` calls.

When you edit the permissions on your default event bus to grant permission to other AWS accounts, you can specify accounts by account ID. Or you can choose to receive events from all AWS accounts.

Warning
If you choose to receive events from all AWS accounts, be careful to create rules that match only events you want to receive from others. To create more secure rules, be sure the event pattern for each rule contains an `account` field with the account IDs of one or more accounts that you want to receive events from. Rules that have an event pattern containing an account field do not match events sent from other accounts. For more information, see Event Patterns in CloudWatch Events.

To enable your account to receive events from other AWS accounts using the console

1. Open the CloudWatch console at https://console.aws.amazon.com/cloudwatch/.

2. In the navigation pane, choose **Event Buses, Add Permission**.

3. For **Principal**, type the 12-digit AWS Account ID of the account from which to receive events. To receive events from all other AWS accounts, choose **Everybody(*)**.

4. Choose **Add**.

To enable your account to receive events from other AWS accounts using the AWS CLI

1. To enable one specific AWS account to send events, run the following command:

```
1 aws events put-permission --action events:PutEvents --statement-id MySid --principal
    SenderAccountID
```

To enable all other AWS accounts to send events, run the following command:

```
1 aws events put-permission --action events:PutEvents --statement-id MySid --principal \*
```

2. After setting permissions for your default event bus, you can optionally use the `describe-event-bus` command to check the permissions.

```
1 aws events describe-event-bus
```

Sending Events to Another AWS Account

To send events to another account, you configure a CloudWatch Events rule that has the default event bus of another AWS account as the target. The default event bus of that receiving account must also be configured to receive events from your account.

To send events from your account to another AWS account using the console

1. Open the CloudWatch console at https://console.aws.amazon.com/cloudwatch/.

2. In the navigation pane, choose **Events, Create Rule**.

3. For **Event Source**, choose **Event Pattern**, and then choose the service name and event types to send to the other account.

4. Choose **Add Target**.

5. In the drop-down list, select **Event bus in another AWS account**. Then in **Account ID**, type the 12-digit account ID of the AWS account to which to send events.

6. At the bottom of the page, choose **Configure Details**.

7. Type a name and description for the rule, and choose **Create Rule **.

To send events to another AWS account using the AWS CLI

1. Use the `put-rule` command to create a rule that matches the event types to send to the other account.

2. Add the other account's default event bus as the target of the rule:

```
1 aws events put-targets --rule NameOfRuleMatchingEventsToSend --targets "Id"="MyId","Arn"="
    arn:aws:events:region:$ReceiverAccountID:event-bus/default"
```

Writing Rules that Match Events from Another AWS Account

If your account is set up to receive events from other AWS accounts, you can write rules that match those events. Set the event pattern of the rule to match the events you are receiving from the other account.

Unless you specify `Account` in the event pattern of a rule, any of your account's rules, both new and existing, that match events you receive from other accounts will trigger based on those events. If you are receiving events from another account, and you want a rule to trigger only on that event pattern when it is generated from your own account, you must add `Account` and specify your own account ID to the event pattern of the rule.

If you set up your AWS account to accept events from all AWS accounts, we strongly recommend that you add `Account` to every CloudWatch Events rule in your account. This prevents rules in your account from triggering on events from unknown AWS accounts. When you specify the `Account` field in the rule, you can specify the account IDs of more than one AWS account in the field.

To write a rule matching events from another account using the console

1. Open the CloudWatch console at https://console.aws.amazon.com/cloudwatch/.

2. In the navigation pane, choose **Events, Create Rule**.

3. For **Event Source**, choose **Event Pattern**, and select the service name and event types that the rule should match.

4. Near **Event Pattern Preview**, choose **Edit**.

5. In the edit window, add an `Account` line specifying what AWS accounts that send this event should be matched by the rule. For example, the edit window originally shows the following:

```
1 {
2   "source": [
3     "aws.ec2"
4   ],
5   "detail-type": [
6     "EBS Volume Notification"
7   ]
8 }
```

You could add the following to make the rule match EBS volume notifications that are sent by the AWS accounts 123456789012 and 111122223333:

```
1  {
2    "account": [
3      "123456789012","111122223333"
4    ],
5    "source": [
6      "aws.ec2"
7    ],
8    "detail-type": [
9      "EBS Volume Notification"
10   ]
11 }
```

6. After editing the event pattern, choose **Save**.

7. Finish creating the rule as usual, setting one or more targets in your account.

To write a rule matching events from another AWS account using the AWS CLI

- Use the `put-rule` command and specify the other AWS accounts that the rule is to match in the `Account` field in the rule's event pattern. The following example rule matches Amazon EC2 instance state changes in the AWS accounts 123456789012 and 111122223333:

```
1 aws events put-rule --name "EC2InstanceStateChanges" --event-pattern "{\"account
    \":["123456789012", "111122223333"],\"source\":[\"aws.ec2\"],\"detail-type\":[\"EC2
    Instance State-change Notification\"]}"  --role-arn "arn:aws:iam::123456789012:role/
    MyRoleForThisRule"
```

Adding Events with PutEvents

The PutEvents action sends multiple events to CloudWatch Events in a single request. For more information, see PutEvents in the *Amazon CloudWatch Events API Reference* and put-events in the *AWS CLI Command Reference*.

Each PutEvents request can support a limited number of entries. For more information, see CloudWatch Events Limits. The PutEvents operation attempts to process all entries in the natural order of the request. Each event has a unique id that is assigned by CloudWatch Events after you call PutEvents.

The following example Java code sends two identical events to CloudWatch Events:

```java
PutEventsRequestEntry requestEntry = new PutEventsRequestEntry()
        .withTime(new Date())
        .withSource("com.mycompany.myapp")
        .withDetailType("myDetailType")
        .withResources("resource1", "resource2")
        .withDetail("{ \"key1\": \"value1\", \"key2\": \"value2\" }");

PutEventsRequest request = new PutEventsRequest()
        .withEntries(requestEntry, requestEntry);

PutEventsResult result = awsEventsClient.putEvents(request);

for (PutEventsResultEntry resultEntry : result.getEntries()) {
    if (resultEntry.getEventId() != null) {
        System.out.println("Event Id: " + resultEntry.getEventId());
    } else {
        System.out.println("Injection failed with Error Code: " + resultEntry.getErrorCode());
    }
}
```

The PutEvents result includes an array of response entries. Each entry in the response array directly correlates with an entry in the request array using natural ordering, from the top to the bottom of the request and response. The response Entries array always includes the same number of entries as the request array.

Handling Failures When Using PutEvents

By default, failure of individual entries within a request does not stop the processing of subsequent entries in the request. This means that a response Entries array includes both successfully and unsuccessfully processed entries. You must detect unsuccessfully processed entries and include them in a subsequent call.

Successful result entries include Id value, and unsuccessful result entries include ErrorCode and ErrorMessage values. The ErrorCode parameter reflects the type of error. ErrorMessage provides more detailed information about the error. The example below has three result entries for a PutEvents request. The second entry has failed and is reflected in the response.

Example: PutEvents Response Syntax

```json
{
    "FailedEntryCount": 1,
    "Entries": [
        {
            "EventId": "11710aed-b79e-4468-a20b-bb3c0c3b4860"
        },
        {   "ErrorCode": "InternalFailure",
```

```
8              "ErrorMessage": "Internal Service Failure"
9         },
10             "EventId": "d804d26a-88db-4b66-9eaf-9a11c708ae82"
11        }
12     ]
13 }
```

Entries that were unsuccessfully processed can be included in subsequent PutEvents requests. First, check the FailedRecordCount parameter in the PutEventsResult to confirm if there are failed records in the request. If so, each Entry that has an ErrorCode that is not null should be added to a subsequent request. For an example of this type of handler, refer to the following code.

Example: PutEvents failure handler

```
1  PutEventsRequestEntry requestEntry = new PutEventsRequestEntry()
2         .withTime(new Date())
3         .withSource("com.mycompany.myapp")
4         .withDetailType("myDetailType")
5         .withResources("resource1", "resource2")
6         .withDetail("{ \"key1\": \"value1\", \"key2\": \"value2\" }");
7
8  List<PutEventsRequestEntry> putEventsRequestEntryList = new ArrayList<>();
9  for (int i = 0; i < 3; i++) {
10     putEventsRequestEntryList.add(requestEntry);
11 }
12
13 PutEventsRequest putEventsRequest = new PutEventsRequest();
14 putEventsRequest.withEntries(putEventsRequestEntryList);
15 PutEventsResult putEventsResult = awsEventsClient.putEvents(putEventsRequest);
16
17 while (putEventsResult.getFailedEntryCount() > 0) {
18     final List<PutEventsRequestEntry> failedEntriesList = new ArrayList<>();
19     final List<PutEventsResultEntry> PutEventsResultEntryList = putEventsResult.getEntries();
20     for (int i = 0; i < PutEventsResultEntryList.size(); i++) {
21         final PutEventsRequestEntry putEventsRequestEntry = putEventsRequestEntryList.get(i);
22         final PutEventsResultEntry putEventsResultEntry = PutEventsResultEntryList.get(i);
23         if (putEventsResultEntry.getErrorCode() != null) {
24             failedEntriesList.add(putEventsRequestEntry);
25         }
26     }
27     putEventsRequestEntryList = failedEntriesList;
28     putEventsRequest.setEntries(putEventsRequestEntryList);
29     putEventsResult = awsEventsClient.putEvents(putEventsRequest);
30 }
```

Sending Events Using the AWS CLI

You can use the AWS CLI to send custom events. The following example puts one custom event into CloudWatch Events:

```
1 aws events put-events \
2 --entries '[{"Time": "2016-01-14T01:02:03Z", "Source": "com.mycompany.myapp", "Resources": ["
    resource1", "resource2"], "DetailType": "myDetailType", "Detail": "{ \"key1\": \"value1\",
    \"key2\": \"value2\" }"}]'
```

You can also create a file for example, **entries.json**, like the following:

```
1  [
2    {
3      "Time": "2016-01-14T01:02:03Z",
4      "Source": "com.mycompany.myapp",
5      "Resources": [
6        "resource1",
7        "resource2"
8      ],
9      "DetailType": "myDetailType",
10     "Detail": "{ \"key1\": \"value1\", \"key2\": \"value2\" }"
11   }
12 ]
```

You can use the AWS CLI to read the entries from this file and send events. At a command prompt, type:

```
1 aws events put-events --entries file://entries.json
```

Calculating PutEvents Event Entry Sizes

You can inject custom events into CloudWatch Events using the `PutEvents` action. You can inject multiple events using the `PutEvents` action as long as the total entry size is less than 256KB. You can calculate the event entry size beforehand by following the steps below. You can then batch multiple event entries into one request for efficiency.

Note

The size limit is imposed on the entry. Even if the entry is less than the size limit, it does not mean that the event in CloudWatch Events is also less than this size. On the contrary, the event size is always larger than the entry size due to the necessary characters and keys of the JSON representation of the event. For more information, see Event Patterns in CloudWatch Events.

The `PutEventsRequestEntry` size is calculated as follows:

- If the `Time` parameter is specified, it is measured as 14 bytes.
- The `Source` and `DetailType` parameters are measured as the number of bytes for their UTF-8 encoded forms.
- If the `Detail` parameter is specified, it is measured as the number of bytes for its UTF-8 encoded form.
- If the `Resources` parameter is specified, each entry is measured as the number of bytes for their UTF-8 encoded forms.

The following example Java code calculates the size of a given `PutEventsRequestEntry` object:

```
 1  int getSize(PutEventsRequestEntry entry) {
 2      int size = 0;
 3      if (entry.getTime() != null) {
 4          size += 14;
 5      }
 6      size += entry.getSource().getBytes(StandardCharsets.UTF_8).length;
 7      size += entry.getDetailType().getBytes(StandardCharsets.UTF_8).length;
 8      if (entry.getDetail() != null) {
 9          size += entry.getDetail().getBytes(StandardCharsets.UTF_8).length;
10      }
11      if (entry.getResources() != null) {
12          for (String resource : entry.getResources()) {
13              if (resource != null) {
14                  size += resource.getBytes(StandardCharsets.UTF_8).length;
15              }
16          }
17      }
18      return size;
19  }
```

Authentication and Access Control for Amazon CloudWatch Events

Access to Amazon CloudWatch Events requires credentials that AWS can use to authenticate your requests. Those credentials must have permissions to access AWS resources, such as retrieving event data from other AWS resources. The following sections provide details on how you can use AWS Identity and Access Management (IAM) and CloudWatch Events to help secure your resources by controlling who can access them:

- Authentication
- Access Control

Authentication

You can access AWS as any of the following types of identities:

- **AWS account root user** – When you sign up for AWS, you provide an email address and password that is associated with your AWS account. These are your *root credentials* and they provide complete access to all of your AWS resources. **Important**
  For security reasons, we recommend that you use the root credentials only to create an *administrator*, which is an *IAM user* with full permissions to your AWS account. Then, you can use this administrator to create other IAM users and roles with limited permissions. For more information, see IAM Best Practices and Creating an Admin User and Group in the *IAM User Guide*.

- **IAM user** – An IAM user is an identity within your AWS account that has specific custom permissions (for example, permissions to send event data to a target in CloudWatch Events). You can use an IAM user name and password to sign in to secure AWS webpages like the AWS Management Console, AWS Discussion Forums, or the AWS Support Center.

  In addition to a user name and password, you can also generate access keys for each user. You can use these keys when you access AWS services programmatically, either through one of the several SDKs or by using the AWS Command Line Interface (AWS CLI). The SDK and AWS CLI tools use the access keys to cryptographically sign your request. If you don't use the AWS tools, you must sign the request yourself. CloudWatch Events supports *Signature Version 4*, a protocol for authenticating inbound API requests. For more information about authenticating requests, see Signature Version 4 Signing Process in the *AWS General Reference*.

- **IAM role** – An IAM role is another IAM identity you can create in your account that has specific permissions. It is similar to an *IAM user*, but it is not associated with a specific person. An IAM role enables you to obtain temporary access keys that can be used to access AWS services and resources. IAM roles with temporary credentials are useful in the following situations:

  - **Federated user access** – Instead of creating an IAM user, you can use preexisting identities from AWS Directory Service, your enterprise user directory, or a web identity provider (IdP). These are known as *federated users*. AWS assigns a role to a federated user when access is requested through an identity provider. For more information about federated users, see Federated Users and Roles in the *IAM User Guide*.

  - **Cross-account access** – You can use an IAM role in your account to grant another AWS account permissions to access your account's resources. For an example, see Tutorial: Delegate Access Across AWS Accounts Using IAM Roles in the *IAM User Guide*.

- **AWS service access** – You can use an IAM role in your account to grant to an AWS service the permissions needed to access your account's resources. For example, you can create a role that allows Amazon Redshift to access an Amazon S3 bucket on your behalf and then load data stored in the bucket into an Amazon Redshift cluster. For more information, see Creating a Role to Delegate Permissions to an AWS Service in the *IAM User Guide*.

- **Applications running on Amazon EC2** – Instead of storing access keys within the EC2 instance for use by applications running on the instance and making AWS API requests, you can use an IAM role to manage temporary credentials for these applications. To assign an AWS role to an EC2 instance and make it available to all of its applications, you can create an instance profile that is attached to the instance. An instance profile contains the role and enables programs running on the EC2 instance to get temporary credentials. For more information, see Using Roles for Applications on Amazon EC2 in the *IAM User Guide*.

Access Control

You can have valid credentials to authenticate your requests, but unless you have permissions you cannot create or access CloudWatch Events resources. For example, you must have permissions to invoke AWS Lambda, Amazon Simple Notification Service (Amazon SNS), and Amazon Simple Queue Service (Amazon SQS) targets associated with your CloudWatch Events rules.

The following sections describe how to manage permissions for CloudWatch Events. We recommend that you read the overview first.

- Overview of Managing Access Permissions to Your CloudWatch Events Resources
- Using Identity-Based Policies (IAM Policies) for CloudWatch Events
- Using Resource-Based Policies for CloudWatch Events
- CloudWatch Events Permissions Reference

Overview of Managing Access Permissions to Your CloudWatch Events Resources

Every AWS resource is owned by an AWS account, and permissions to create or access a resource are governed by permissions policies. An account administrator can attach permissions policies to IAM identities (that is, users, groups, and roles), and some services (such as AWS Lambda) also support attaching permissions policies to resources.

Note

An *account administrator* (or administrator IAM user) is a user with administrator privileges. For more information, see IAM Best Practices in the *IAM User Guide*.

When granting permissions, you decide who is getting the permissions, the resources they get permissions for, and the specific actions that you want to allow on those resources.

Topics

- CloudWatch Events Resources and Operations
- Understanding Resource Ownership
- Managing Access to Resources
- Specifying Policy Elements: Actions, Effects, and Principals
- Specifying Conditions in a Policy

CloudWatch Events Resources and Operations

In CloudWatch Events, the primary resource is a rule. CloudWatch Events supports other resources that can be used with the primary resource, such as events. These are referred to as subresources. These resources and subresources have unique Amazon Resource Names (ARNs) associated with them. For more information about ARNs, see Amazon Resource Names (ARN) and AWS Service Namespaces in the *Amazon Web Services General Reference*.

Resource Type	ARN Format
Rule	`arn:aws:events:region:account:rule/rule-name`
All CloudWatch Events resources	`arn:aws:events:*`
All CloudWatch Events resources owned by the specified account in the specified region	`arn:aws:events:region:account:*`

Note

Most services in AWS treat a colon (:) or a forward slash (/) as the same character in ARNs. However, CloudWatch Events uses an exact match in event patterns and rules. Be sure to use the correct ARN characters when creating event patterns so that they match the ARN syntax in the event you want to match.

For example, you can indicate a specific rule (*myRule*) in your statement using its ARN as follows:

```
1 "Resource": "arn:aws:events:us-east-1:123456789012:rule/myRule"
```

You can also specify all rules that belong to a specific account by using the asterisk (*) wildcard as follows:

```
1 "Resource": "arn:aws:events:us-east-1:123456789012:rule/*"
```

To specify all resources, or if a specific API action does not support ARNs, use the asterisk (*) wildcard in the Resource element as follows:

```
1 "Resource": "*"
```

Some CloudWatch Events API actions accept multiple resources (that is, `PutTargets`). To specify multiple resources in a single statement, separate their ARNs with commas, as follows:

```
1  "Resource": ["arn1", "arn2"]
```

CloudWatch Events provides a set of operations to work with the CloudWatch Events resources. For a list of available operations, see CloudWatch Events Permissions Reference.

Understanding Resource Ownership

The AWS account owns the resources that are created in the account, regardless of who created the resources. Specifically, the resource owner is the AWS account of the principal entity (that is, the AWS account root user, an IAM user, or an IAM role) that authenticates the resource creation request. The following examples illustrate how this works:

- If you use the root user credentials of your AWS account to create a rule, your AWS account is the owner of the CloudWatch Events resource.
- If you create an IAM user in your AWS account and grant permissions to create CloudWatch Events resources to that user, the user can create CloudWatch Events resources. However, your AWS account, to which the user belongs, owns the CloudWatch Events resources.
- If you create an IAM role in your AWS account with permissions to create CloudWatch Events resources, anyone who can assume the role can create CloudWatch Events resources. Your AWS account, to which the role belongs, owns the CloudWatch Events resources.

Managing Access to Resources

A *permissions policy* describes who has access to what. The following section explains the available options for creating permissions policies.

Note
This section discusses using IAM in the context of CloudWatch Events. It doesn't provide detailed information about the IAM service. For complete IAM documentation, see What Is IAM? in the *IAM User Guide*. For information about IAM policy syntax and descriptions, see IAM Policy Reference in the *IAM User Guide*.

Policies attached to an IAM identity are referred to as identity-based policies (IAM polices) and policies attached to a resource are referred to as resource-based policies. CloudWatch Events supports both identity-based (IAM policies) and resource-based policies.

Topics

- Identity-Based Policies (IAM Policies)
- Resource-Based Policies (IAM Policies)

Identity-Based Policies (IAM Policies)

You can attach policies to IAM identities. For example, you can do the following:

- **Attach a permissions policy to a user or a group in your account** – To grant a user permissions to view rules in the CloudWatch console, you can attach a permissions policy to a user or group that the user belongs to.

- **Attach a permissions policy to a role (grant cross-account permissions)** – You can attach an identity-based permissions policy to an IAM role to grant cross-account permissions. For example, the administrator in account A can create a role to grant cross-account permissions to another AWS account (for example, account B) or an AWS service as follows:

1. Account A administrator creates an IAM role and attaches a permissions policy to the role that grants permissions on resources in account A.

2. Account A administrator attaches a trust policy to the role identifying account B as the principal who can assume the role.

3. Account B administrator can then delegate permissions to assume the role to any users in account B. Doing this allows users in account B to create or access resources in account A. The principal in the trust policy can also be an AWS service principal to grant to an AWS service the permissions needed to assume the role.

For more information about using IAM to delegate permissions, see Access Management in the *IAM User Guide*.

You can create specific IAM policies to restrict the calls and resources that users in your account have access to, and then attach those policies to IAM users. For more information about how to create IAM roles and to explore example IAM policy statements for CloudWatch Events, see Overview of Managing Access Permissions to Your CloudWatch Events Resources.

Resource-Based Policies (IAM Policies)

When a rule is triggered in CloudWatch Events, all the targets associated with the rule are invoked. *Invocation* means invoking the AWS Lambda functions, publishing to the Amazon SNS topics, and relaying the event to the Kinesis streams. In order to be able to make API calls against the resources you own, CloudWatch Events needs the appropriate permissions. For Lambda, Amazon SNS, and Amazon SQS resources, CloudWatch Events relies on resource-based policies. For Kinesis streams, CloudWatch Events relies on IAM roles.

For more information about how to create IAM roles and to explore example resource-based policy statements for CloudWatch Events, see Using Resource-Based Policies for CloudWatch Events.

Specifying Policy Elements: Actions, Effects, and Principals

For each CloudWatch Events resource, the service defines a set of API operations. To grant permissions for these API operations, CloudWatch Events defines a set of actions that you can specify in a policy. Some API operations can require permissions for more than one action in order to perform the API operation. For more information about resources and API operations, see CloudWatch Events Resources and Operations and CloudWatch Events Permissions Reference.

The following are the basic policy elements:

- **Resource** – You use an Amazon Resource Name (ARN) to identify the resource that the policy applies to. For more information, see CloudWatch Events Resources and Operations.
- **Action** – You use action keywords to identify resource operations that you want to allow or deny. For example, the `events:Describe` permission allows the user permissions to perform the `Describe` operation.
- **Effect** – You specify the effect, either allow or deny, when the user requests the specific action. If you don't explicitly grant access to (allow) a resource, access is implicitly denied. You can also explicitly deny access to a resource, which you might do to make sure that a user cannot access it, even if a different policy grants access.
- **Principal** – In identity-based policies (IAM policies), the user that the policy is attached to is the implicit principal. For resource-based policies, you specify the user, account, service, or other entity that you want to receive permissions (applies to resource-based policies only).

To learn more about IAM policy syntax and descriptions, see AWS IAM Policy Reference in the *IAM User Guide*.

For a table showing all of the CloudWatch Events API actions and the resources that they apply to, see CloudWatch Events Permissions Reference.

Specifying Conditions in a Policy

When you grant permissions, you can use the access policy language to specify the conditions when a policy should take effect. For example, you might want a policy to be applied only after a specific date. For more information about specifying conditions in a policy language, see Condition in the *IAM User Guide*.

To express conditions, you use predefined condition keys. There are AWS-wide condition keys and CloudWatch Events–specific keys that you can use as appropriate. For a complete list of AWS-wide keys, see Available Keys for Conditions in the *IAM User Guide*. For a complete list of CloudWatch Events–specific keys, see Using IAM Policy Conditions for Fine-Grained Access Control.

Using Identity-Based Policies (IAM Policies) for CloudWatch Events

This topic provides examples of identity-based policies in which an account administrator can attach permissions policies to IAM identities (that is, users, groups, and roles).

The following shows an example of a permissions policy that allows a user to put event data into Kinesis.

```
1  {
2      "Version": "2012-10-17",
3      "Statement": [
4          {
5              "Sid": "CloudWatchEventsInvocationAccess",
6              "Effect": "Allow",
7              "Action": [
8                  "kinesis:PutRecord"
9              ],
10             "Resource": "*"
11         }
12     ]
13 }
```

The sections in this topic cover the following:

Topics

- Permissions Required to Use the CloudWatch Console
- AWS Managed (Predefined) Policies for CloudWatch Events
- Permissions Required for CloudWatch Events to Access Certain Targets
- Customer Managed Policy Examples

Permissions Required to Use the CloudWatch Console

For a user to work with CloudWatch Events in the CloudWatch console, that user must have a minimum set of permissions that allow the user to describe other AWS resources for their AWS account. In order to use CloudWatch Events in the CloudWatch console, you must have permissions from the following services:

- Automation
- Amazon EC2 Auto Scaling
- CloudTrail
- CloudWatch
- CloudWatch Events
- IAM
- Kinesis
- Lambda
- Amazon SNS
- Amazon SWF

If you create an IAM policy that is more restrictive than the minimum required permissions, the console won't function as intended for users with that IAM policy. To ensure that those users can still use the CloudWatch console, also attach the `CloudWatchEventsReadOnlyAccess` managed policy to the user, as described in AWS Managed (Predefined) Policies for CloudWatch Events.

You don't need to allow minimum console permissions for users that are making calls only to the AWS CLI or the CloudWatch API.

The full set of permissions required to work with the CloudWatch console are listed below:

- `automation:CreateAction`

- automation:DescribeAction
- automation:UpdateAction
- autoscaling:DescribeAutoScalingGroups
- cloudtrail:DescribeTrails
- ec2:DescribeInstances
- ec2:DescribeVolumes
- events:DeleteRule
- events:DescribeRule
- events:DisableRule
- events:EnableRule
- events:ListRuleNamesByTarget
- events:ListRules
- events:ListTargetsByRule
- events:PutEvents
- events:PutRule
- events:PutTargets
- events:RemoveTargets
- events:TestEventPattern
- iam:ListRoles
- kinesis:ListStreams
- lambda:AddPermission
- lambda:ListFunctions
- lambda:RemovePermission
- sns:GetTopicAttributes
- sns:ListTopics
- sns:SetTopicAttributes
- swf:DescribeAction
- swf:ReferenceAction
- swf:RegisterAction
- swf:RegisterDomain
- swf:UpdateAction

AWS Managed (Predefined) Policies for CloudWatch Events

AWS addresses many common use cases by providing standalone IAM policies that are created and administered by AWS. Managed policies grant necessary permissions for common use cases so you can avoid having to investigate what permissions are needed. For more information, see AWS Managed Policies in the *IAM User Guide*.

The following AWS managed policies, which you can attach to users in your account, are specific to CloudWatch Events:

- **CloudWatchEventsFullAccess** – Grants full access to CloudWatch Events.
- **CloudWatchEventsInvocationAccess** – Allows CloudWatch Events to relay events to the streams in Amazon Kinesis Data Streams in your account.
- **CloudWatchEventsReadOnlyAccess** – Grants read-only access to CloudWatch Events.
- **CloudWatchEventsBuiltInTargetExecutionAccess** – Allows built-in targets in CloudWatch Events to perform Amazon EC2 actions on your behalf.

IAM Roles for Sending Events

In order for CloudWatch Events to relay events to your Kinesis stream targets, you must create an IAM role.

To create an IAM role for sending CloudWatch Events

1. Open the IAM console at https://console.aws.amazon.com/iam/.

2. Follow the steps in Creating a Role to Delegate Permissions to an AWS Service in the *IAM User Guide* to create an IAM role. As you follow the steps to create a role, do the following:

   - In **Role Name**, use a name that is unique within your AWS account (for example, **Cloud-WatchEventsSending**).
   - In **Select Role Type**, choose **AWS Service Roles**, and then choose **Amazon CloudWatch Events**. This grants CloudWatch Events permissions to assume the role.
   - In **Attach Policy**, choose **CloudWatchEventsInvocationAccess**.

You can also create your own custom IAM policies to allow permissions for CloudWatch Events actions and resources. You can attach these custom policies to the IAM users or groups that require those permissions. For more information about IAM policies, see Overview of IAM Policies in the *IAM User Guide*. For more information about managing and creating custom IAM policies, see Managing IAM Policies in the *IAM User Guide*.

Permissions Required for CloudWatch Events to Access Certain Targets

For CloudWatch Events to access certain targets, you must specify an IAM role for accessing that target, and that role must have a certain policy attached.

If the target is a Kinesis stream, the role used to send event data to that target must include the following policy:

```
{
    "Version": "2012-10-17",
    "Statement": [
        {
            "Effect": "Allow",
            "Action": [
                "kinesis:PutRecord"
            ],
            "Resource": "*"
        }
    ]
}
```

If the target is Run Command and you are specifying one or more InstanceIds values for the command, the role that you specify must include the following policy:

```
{
    "Version": "2012-10-17",
    "Statement": [
        {
            "Action": "ssm:SendCommand",
            "Effect": "Allow",
            "Resource": [
                "arn:aws:ec2:{{region}}:{{accountId}}:instance/[[instanceIds]]",
                "arn:aws:ssm:{{region}}:*:document/{{documentName}}"
            ]
        }
    ]
}
```

If the target is Run Command and you are specifying one or more tags for the command, the role that you specify must include the following policy:

```
 1 {
 2     "Version": "2012-10-17",
 3     "Statement": [
 4         {
 5             "Action": "ssm:SendCommand",
 6             "Effect": "Allow",
 7             "Resource": [
 8                 "arn:aws:ec2:{{region}}:{{accountId}}:instance/*"
 9             ],
10             "Condition": {
11                 "StringEquals": {
12                     "ec2:ResourceTag/*": [
13                         "[[tagValues]]"
14                     ]
15                 }
16             }
17         },
18         {
19             "Action": "ssm:SendCommand",
20             "Effect": "Allow",
21             "Resource": [
22                 "arn:aws:ssm:{{region}}:*:document/{{documentName}}"
23             ]
24         }
25     ]
26 }
```

If the target is a Step Functions state machine, the role that you specify must include the following policy:

```
 1 {
 2     "Version": "2012-10-17",
 3     "Statement": [
 4         {
 5             "Effect": "Allow",
 6             "Action": [ "states:StartExecution" ],
 7             "Resource": [ "arn:aws:states:*:*:stateMachine:*" ]
 8         }
 9     ]
10 }
```

If the target is an ECS task, the role that you specify must include the following policy:

```
 1 {
 2     "Version": "2012-10-17",
 3     "Statement": [{
 4         "Effect": "Allow",
 5         "Action": [
 6             "ecs:RunTask"
 7         ],
 8         "Resource": [
 9             "arn:aws:ecs:*:{{account-id}}:task-definition/{{task-definition-name}}"
10         ],
11         "Condition": {
12             "ArnLike": {
13                 "ecs:cluster": "arn:aws:ecs:*:{{account-id}}:cluster/{{cluster-name}}"
14             }
```

```
15        }
16    }]
17 }
```

Customer Managed Policy Examples

In this section, you can find example user policies that grant permissions for various CloudWatch Events actions. These policies work when you are using the CloudWatch Events API, AWS SDKs, or the AWS CLI.

Note
All examples use the US West (Oregon) Region (us-west-2) and contain fictitious account IDs.

You can use the following sample IAM policies listed to limit the CloudWatch Events access for your IAM users and roles.

Topics

- Example 1: CloudWatchEventsBuiltInTargetExecutionAccess
- Example 2: CloudWatchEventsInvocationAccess
- Example 3: CloudWatchEventsConsoleAccess
- Example 4: CloudWatchEventsFullAccess
- Example 5: CloudWatchEventsReadOnlyAccess

Example 1: CloudWatchEventsBuiltInTargetExecutionAccess

The following policy allows built-in targets in CloudWatch Events to perform Amazon EC2 actions on your behalf.

Important
Creating rules with built-in targets is supported only in the AWS Management Console.

```
1 {
2     "Version": "2012-10-17",
3     "Statement": [
4         {
5             "Sid": "CloudWatchEventsBuiltInTargetExecutionAccess",
6             "Effect": "Allow",
7             "Action": [
8                 "ec2:Describe*",
9                 "ec2:RebootInstances",
10                "ec2:StopInstances",
11                "ec2:TerminateInstances",
12                "ec2:CreateSnapshot"
13            ],
14            "Resource": "*"
15        }
16    ]
17 }
```

Example 2: CloudWatchEventsInvocationAccess

The following policy allows CloudWatch Events to relay events to the streams in Kinesis streams in your account.

```
1  {
2      "Version": "2012-10-17",
3      "Statement": [
4          {
5              "Sid": "CloudWatchEventsInvocationAccess",
6              "Effect": "Allow",
7              "Action": [
8                  "kinesis:PutRecord"
9              ],
10             "Resource": "*"
11         }
12     ]
13 }
```

Example 3: CloudWatchEventsConsoleAccess

The following policy ensures that IAM users can use the CloudWatch Events console.

```
1  {
2      "Version": "2012-10-17",
3      "Statement": [
4          {
5              "Sid": "CloudWatchEventsConsoleAccess",
6              "Effect": "Allow",
7              "Action": [
8                  "automation:CreateAction",
9                  "automation:DescribeAction",
10                 "automation:UpdateAction",
11                 "autoscaling:DescribeAutoScalingGroups",
12                 "cloudtrail:DescribeTrails",
13                 "ec2:DescribeInstances",
14                 "ec2:DescribeVolumes",
15                 "events:*",
16                 "iam:ListRoles",
17                 "kinesis:ListStreams",
18                 "lambda:AddPermission",
19                 "lambda:ListFunctions",
20                 "lambda:RemovePermission",
21                 "sns:GetTopicAttributes",
22                 "sns:ListTopics",
23                 "sns:SetTopicAttributes",
24                 "swf:DescribeAction",
25                 "swf:ReferenceAction",
26                 "swf:RegisterAction",
27                 "swf:RegisterDomain",
28                 "swf:UpdateAction"
29             ],
30             "Resource": "*"
31         },
32         {
33             "Sid": "IAMPassRoleForCloudWatchEvents",
34             "Effect": "Allow",
35             "Action": "iam:PassRole",
36             "Resource": [
```

```
37              "arn:aws:iam::*:role/AWS_Events_Invoke_Targets",
38              "arn:aws:iam::*:role/AWS_Events_Actions_Execution"
39          ]
40      }
41    ]
42 }
```

Example 4: CloudWatchEventsFullAccess

The following policy allows performing actions against CloudWatch Events through the AWS CLI and SDK.

```
1 {
2     "Version": "2012-10-17",
3     "Statement": [
4         {
5             "Sid": "CloudWatchEventsFullAccess",
6             "Effect": "Allow",
7             "Action": "events:*",
8             "Resource": "*"
9         },
10        {
11            "Sid": "IAMPassRoleForCloudWatchEvents",
12            "Effect": "Allow",
13            "Action": "iam:PassRole",
14            "Resource": "arn:aws:iam::*:role/AWS_Events_Invoke_Targets"
15        }
16    ]
17 }
```

Example 5: CloudWatchEventsReadOnlyAccess

The following policy provides read-only access to CloudWatch Events.

```
1 {
2     "Version": "2012-10-17",
3     "Statement": [
4         {
5             "Sid": "CloudWatchEventsReadOnlyAccess",
6             "Effect": "Allow",
7             "Action": [
8                 "events:Describe*",
9                 "events:List*",
10                "events:TestEventPattern"
11            ],
12            "Resource": "*"
13        }
14    ]
15 }
```

Using Resource-Based Policies for CloudWatch Events

When a rule is triggered in CloudWatch Events, all the targets associated with the rule are invoked. *Invocation* means invoking the AWS Lambda functions, publishing to the Amazon SNS topics, and relaying the event to the Kinesis streams. In order to be able to make API calls against the resources you own, CloudWatch Events needs the appropriate permissions. For Lambda, Amazon SNS, and Amazon SQS resources, CloudWatch Events relies on resource-based policies. For Kinesis streams, CloudWatch Events relies on IAM roles.

You can use the following permissions to invoke the targets associated with your CloudWatch Events rules. The procedures below use the AWS CLI to add permissions to your targets. For information about how to install and configure the AWS CLI, see Getting Set Up with the AWS Command Line Interface in the *AWS Command Line Interface User Guide*.

Topics

- AWS Lambda Permissions
- Amazon SNS Permissions
- Amazon SQS Permissions

AWS Lambda Permissions

To invoke your AWS Lambda function using a CloudWatch Events rule, add the following permission to the policy of your Lambda function.

```
1  {
2    "Effect": "Allow",
3    "Action": "lambda:InvokeFunction",
4    "Resource": "arn:aws:lambda:region:account-id:function:function-name",
5    "Principal": {
6      "Service": "events.amazonaws.com"
7    },
8    "Condition": {
9      "ArnLike": {
10       "AWS:SourceArn": "arn:aws:events:region:account-id:rule/rule-name"
11     }
12   },
13   "Sid": "TrustCWEToInvokeMyLambdaFunction"
14 }
```

To add permissions that enable CloudWatch Events to invoke Lambda functions

- At a command prompt, enter the following command:

```
1  aws lambda add-permission --statement-id "TrustCWEToInvokeMyLambdaFunction" \
2  --action "lambda:InvokeFunction" \
3  --principal "events.amazonaws.com" \
4  --function-name "arn:aws:lambda:region:account-id:function:function-name" \
5  --source-arn "arn:aws:events:region:account-id:rule/rule-name"
```

For more information about setting permissions that enable CloudWatch Events to invoke Lambda functions, see AddPermission and Using Lambda with Scheduled Events in the *AWS Lambda Developer Guide*.

Amazon SNS Permissions

To allow CloudWatch Events to publish an Amazon SNS topic, use the `aws sns get-topic-attributes` and the `aws sns set-topic-attributes` commands.

To add permissions that enable CloudWatch Events to publish SNS topics

1. First, list SNS topic attributes. At a command prompt, type the following:

```
1 aws sns get-topic-attributes --topic-arn "arn:aws:sns:region:account-id:topic-name"
```

The command returns all attributes of the SNS topic. The following example shows the result of a newly created SNS topic.

```
1  {
2      "Attributes": {
3          "SubscriptionsConfirmed": "0",
4          "DisplayName": "",
5          "SubscriptionsDeleted": "0",
6          "EffectiveDeliveryPolicy": "{\"http\":{\"defaultHealthyRetryPolicy\":{\"
              minDelayTarget\":20,\"maxDelayTarget\":20,\"numRetries\":3,\"numMaxDelayRetries
              \":0,\"numNoDelayRetries\":0,\"numMinDelayRetries\":0,\"backoffFunction\":\"
              linear\"},\"disableSubscriptionOverrides\":false}}",
7          "Owner": "account-id",
8          "Policy": "{\"Version\":\"2012-10-17\",\"Id\":\"__default_policy_ID\",\"Statement
              \":[{\"Sid\":\"__default_statement_ID\",\"Effect\":\"Allow\",\"Principal\":{\"
              AWS\":\"*\"},\"Action\":[\"SNS:GetTopicAttributes\",\"SNS:SetTopicAttributes
              \",\"SNS:AddPermission\",\"SNS:RemovePermission\",\"SNS:DeleteTopic\",\"SNS:
              Subscribe\",\"SNS:ListSubscriptionsByTopic\",\"SNS:Publish\",\"SNS:Receive
              \"],\"Resource\":\"arn:aws:sns:region:account-id:topic-name\",\"Condition\":{\"
              StringEquals\":{\"AWS:SourceOwner\":\"account-id\"}}}]}",
9          "TopicArn": "arn:aws:sns:region:account-id:topic-name",
10         "SubscriptionsPending": "0"
11     }
12 }
```

2. Next, convert the following statement to a string and add it to the "Statement" collection inside the "Policy" attribute.

```
1  {
2    "Sid": "TrustCWEToPublishEventsToMyTopic",
3    "Effect": "Allow",
4    "Principal": {
5      "Service": "events.amazonaws.com"
6    },
7    "Action": "sns:Publish",
8    "Resource": "arn:aws:sns:region:account-id:topic-name"
9  }
```

After you convert the statement to a string, it should look like the following:

```
1 {\"Sid\":\"TrustCWEToPublishEventsToMyTopic\",\"Effect\":\"Allow\",\"Principal\":{\"Service
      \":\"events.amazonaws.com\"},\"Action\":\"sns:Publish\",\"Resource\":\"arn:aws:sns:
      region:account-id:topic-name\"}
```

3. After you've added the statement string to the statement collection, use the `aws sns set-topic-attributes` command to set the new policy.

```
1 aws sns set-topic-attributes --topic-arn "arn:aws:sns:region:account-id:topic-name" \
2 --attribute-name Policy \
3 --attribute-value "{\"Version\":\"2012-10-17\",\"Id\":\"__default_policy_ID\",\"Statement
      \":[{\"Sid\":\"__default_statement_ID\",\"Effect\":\"Allow\",\"Principal\":{\"AWS
      \":\"*\"},\"Action\":[\"SNS:GetTopicAttributes\",\"SNS:SetTopicAttributes\",\"SNS:
```

```
AddPermission\",\"SNS:RemovePermission\",\"SNS:DeleteTopic\",\"SNS:Subscribe\",\"SNS:
ListSubscriptionsByTopic\",\"SNS:Publish\",\"SNS:Receive\"],\"Resource\":\"arn:aws:sns:
region:account-id:topic-name\",\"Condition\":{\"StringEquals\":{\"AWS:SourceOwner\":\"
account-id\"}}}, {\"Sid\":\"TrustCWEToPublishEventsToMyTopic\",\"Effect\":\"Allow\",\"
Principal\":{\"Service\":\"events.amazonaws.com\"},\"Action\":\"sns:Publish\",\"
Resource\":\"arn:aws:sns:region:account-id:topic-name\"}]}"
```

For more information, see the SetTopicAttributes action in the *Amazon Simple Notification Service API Reference*.

Amazon SQS Permissions

To allow a CloudWatch Events rule to invoke an Amazon SQS queue, use the `aws sqs get-queue-attributes` and the `aws sqs set-queue-attributes` commands.

To add permissions that enable CloudWatch Events rules to invoke an SQS queue

1. First, list SQS queue attributes. At a command prompt, type the following:

```
1 aws sqs get-queue-attributes \
2 --queue-url https://sqs.region.amazonaws.com/account-id/queue-name \
3 --attribute-names Policy
```

   For a newly created SQS queue, its policy is empty by default. In addition to adding a statement, you also need to create a policy that contains this statement.

2. The following statement enables CloudWatch Events to send messages to an SQS queue:

```
1  {
2    "Sid": "TrustCWEToSendEventsToMyQueue",
3    "Effect": "Allow",
4    "Principal": {
5      "Service": "events.amazonaws.com"
6    },
7    "Action": "sqs:SendMessage",
8    "Resource": "arn:aws:sqs:region:account-id:queue-name",
9    "Condition": {
10     "ArnEquals": {
11       "aws:SourceArn": "arn:aws:events:region:account-id:rule/rule-name"
12     }
13   }
14 }
```

3. Next, convert the preceding statement into a string. After you convert the policy to a string, it should look like the following:

```
1 {\"Sid\": \"TrustCWEToSendEventsToMyQueue\", \"Effect\": \"Allow\", \"Principal\": {\"AWS
  \": \"events.amazonaws.com\"}, \"Action\": \"sqs:SendMessage\", \"Resource\": \"arn:aws
  :sqs:region:account-id:queue-name\", \"Condition\": {\"ArnEquals\": {\"aws:SourceArn\":
  \"arn:aws:events:region:account-id:rule/rule-name\"}}
```

4. Create a file called **set-queue-attributes.json** with the following content:

```
1 {
2   "Policy": "{\"Version\":\"2012-10-17\",\"Id\":\"arn:aws:sqs:region:account-id:queue-
      name/SQSDefaultPolicy\",\"Statement\":[{\"Sid\": \"TrustCWEToSendEventsToMyQueue\",
      \"Effect\": \"Allow\", \"Principal\": {\"AWS\": \"events.amazonaws.com\"}, \"
      Action\": \"sqs:SendMessage\", \"Resource\": \"arn:aws:sqs:region:account-id:queue-
      name\", \"Condition\": {\"ArnEquals\": {\"aws:SourceArn\": \"arn:aws:events:region:
      account-id:rule/rule-name\"}}}]}"
```

```
3 }
```

5. Set the policy attribute using the set-queue-attributes.json file as the input. At a command prompt, type:

```
1 aws sqs set-queue-attributes \
2 --queue-url https://sqs.region.amazonaws.com/account-id/queue-name \
3 --attributes file://set-queue-attributes.json
```

If the SQS queue already has a policy, you need to copy the original policy and combine it with a new statement in the set-queue-attributes.json file and run the preceding command to update the policy.

For more information, see Amazon SQS Policy Examples in the *Amazon Simple Queue Service Developer Guide*.

CloudWatch Events Permissions Reference

When you are setting up Access Control and writing permissions policies that you can attach to an IAM identity (identity-based policies), you can use the following table as a reference. The table lists each CloudWatch Events API operation and the corresponding actions for which you can grant permissions to perform the action. You specify the actions in the policy's `Action` field, and you specify a wildcard character (*) as the resource value in the policy's `Resource` field.

You can use AWS-wide condition keys in your CloudWatch Events policies to express conditions. For a complete list of AWS-wide keys, see Available Keys in the *IAM User Guide*.

Note

To specify an action, use the `events:` prefix followed by the API operation name. For example: `events:PutRule`, `events:EnableRule`, or `events:*` (for all CloudWatch Events actions).

To specify multiple actions in a single statement, separate them with commas as follows:

```
1  "Action": ["events:action1", "events:action2"]
```

You can also specify multiple actions using wildcards. For example, you can specify all actions whose name begins with the word "Put" as follows:

```
1  "Action": "events:Put*"
```

To specify all CloudWatch Events API actions, use the * wildcard as follows:

```
1  "Action": "events:*"
```

The actions you can specify in an IAM policy for use with CloudWatch Events are listed below.

CloudWatch Events API Operations and Required Permissions for Actions

CloudWatch Events API Operations	Required Permissions (API Actions)
DeleteRule	`events:DeleteRule` Required to delete a rule.
DescribeEventBus	`events:DescribeEventBus` Required to list AWS accounts that are allowed to write events to the current account's event bus.
DescribeRule	`events:DescribeRule` Required to list the details about a rule.
DisableRule	`events:DisableRule` Required to disable a rule.
EnableRule	`events:EnableRule` Required to enable a rule.
ListRuleNamesByTarget	`events:ListRuleNamesByTarget` Required to list rules associated with a target.
ListRules	`events:ListRules` Required to list all rules in your account.
ListTargetsByRule	`events:ListTargetsByRule` Required to list all targets associated with a rule.
PutEvents	`events:PutEvents` Required to add custom events that can be matched to rules.
PutPermission	`events:PutPermission` Required to give another account permission to write events to this account's default event bus.
PutRule	`events:PutRule` Required to create or update a rule.

CloudWatch Events API Operations	Required Permissions (API Actions)
PutTargets	`events:PutTargets` Required to add targets to a rule.
RemovePermission	`events:RemovePermission` Required to revoke another account's permissions for writing events to this account's default event bus.
RemoveTargets	`events:RemoveTargets` Required to remove a target from a rule.
TestEventPattern	`events:TestEventPattern` Required to test an event pattern against a given event.

Using IAM Policy Conditions for Fine-Grained Access Control

When you grant permissions, you can use the IAM policy language to specify the conditions when a policy should take effect. In a policy statement, you can optionally specify conditions that control when it is in effect. Each condition contains one or more key-value pairs. Condition keys are not case-sensitive. For example, you might want a policy to be applied only after a specific date.

If you specify multiple conditions, or multiple keys in a single condition, they are evaluated using a logical AND operation. If you specify a single condition with multiple values for one key, they are evaluated using a logical OR operation. For permission to be granted, all conditions must be met.

You can also use placeholders when you specify conditions. For more information, see Policy Variables in the *IAM User Guide.* For more information about specifying conditions in an IAM policy language, see Condition in the *IAM User Guide.*

By default, IAM users and roles can't access the events in your account. To consume events, a user must be authorized for the `PutRule` API action. If you allow an IAM user or role for the `events:PutRule` action in their policy, then they will be able to create a rule that matches certain events. You must add a target to a rule, otherwise, a rule without a target does nothing except publish a CloudWatch metric when it matches an incoming event. Your IAM user or role must have permissions for the `events:PutTargets` action.

It is possible to limit access to the events by scoping the authorization to specific sources and types of events (using the `events:source` and `events:detail-type` condition keys). You can provide a condition in the policy statement of the IAM user or role that allows them to create a rule that only matches a specific set of sources and detail types. For a list showing all of condition key values and the CloudWatch Events actions and resources that they apply to, see Using IAM Policy Conditions for Fine-Grained Access Control.

Similarly, through setting conditions in your policy statements, you can decide which specific resources in your accounts can be added to a rule by an IAM user or role (using the `events:TargetArn` condition key). For example, if you turn on CloudTrail in your account and you have a CloudTrail stream, CloudTrail events are also available to the users in your account through CloudWatch Events. If you want your users to use CloudWatch Events and access all the events but the CloudTrail events, you can add a deny statement on the `PutRule` API action with a condition that any rule created by that user or role cannot match the CloudTrail event type.

For CloudTrail events, you can limit the access to a specific principal that the original API call was originated from (using the `events:detail.userIdentity.principalId` condition key). For example, you can allow a user to see all the CloudTrail events, except the ones that are made by a specific IAM role in your account that you use for auditing or forensics.

Condition Key	Key/Value Pair	Evaluation Types
`events:source`	`"events:source":"source"` Where *source* is the literal string for the source field of the event such as `"aws.ec2"` and `"aws.s3"`. To see more possible values for *source*, see the example events in CloudWatch Events Event Examples From Each Supported Service.	Source, Null

Condition Key	Key/Value Pair	Evaluation Types
`events:detail-type`	`"events:detail-type":"` `detail-type "` Where *detail-type* is the literal string for the **detail-type** field of the event such as `"AWS API Call via CloudTrail"` and `"EC2 Instance State-change Notification"`. To see more possible values for *detail-type*, see the example events in CloudWatch Events Event Examples From Each Supported Service.	Detail Type, Null
`events: detail. userIdentity.principalId`	`"events: detail. userIdentity.principalId ":"principal-id"` Where *principal-id* is the literal string for the **detail.userIdentity.principalId** field of the event with detail-type "AWS API Call via CloudTrail" such as `"AROAIDPPEZS35WEXAMPLE: AssumedRoleSessionName."`.	Principal Id, Null
`events:TargetArn`	`"events:TargetArn":"` `target-arn "` Where *target-arn* is the ARN of the target that can be put to a rule such as `"arn:aws:lambda:*:*: function:*"`.	ARN, Null

For example policy statements for CloudWatch Events, see Overview of Managing Access Permissions to Your CloudWatch Events Resources.

Topics

- Example 1: Limit Access to a Specific Source
- Example 2: Define Multiple Sources That Can Be Used in an Event Pattern Individually
- Example 3: Define a Source and a DetailType That Can Be Used in an Event Pattern
- Example 4: Ensure That the Source Is Defined in the Event Pattern
- Example 5: Define a List of Allowed Sources in an Event Pattern with Multiple Sources
- Example 6: Ensure That AWS CloudTrail Events for API Calls from a Certain PrincipalId Are Consumed
- Example 7: Limiting Access to Targets

Example 1: Limit Access to a Specific Source

The following example policies can be attached to an IAM user. Policy A allows the `PutRule` API action for all events, whereas Policy B allows `PutRule` only if the event pattern of the rule being created matches Amazon EC2 events.

Policy A:—allow any events

```
1 {
```

```
2        "Version": "2012-10-17",
3        "Statement": [
4            {
5                "Sid": "AllowPutRuleForAllEvents",
6                "Effect": "Allow",
7                "Action": "events:PutRule",
8                "Resource": "*"
9            }
10       ]
11   }
```

Policy B:—allow events only from Amazon EC2

```
1  {
2        "Version": "2012-10-17",
3        "Statement": [
4            {
5                "Sid": "AllowPutRuleForAllEC2Events",
6                "Effect": "Allow",
7                "Action": "events:PutRule",
8                "Resource": "*",
9                "Condition": {
10                   "StringEquals": {
11                       "events:source": "aws.ec2"
12                   }
13               }
14           }
15       ]
16 }
```

EventPattern is a mandatory argument to `PutRule`. Hence, if the user with Policy B calls `PutRule` with an event pattern like the following:

```
1  {
2        "source": [ "aws.ec2" ]
3  }
```

The rule would be created because the policy allows for this specific source, that is, "aws.ec2". However, if the user with Policy B calls `PutRule` with an event pattern like the following:

```
1  {
2        "source": [ "aws.s3" ]
3  }
```

The rule creation would be denied because the policy does not allow for this specific source, that is, "aws.s3". Essentially, the user with Policy B is only allowed to create a rule that would match the events originating from Amazon EC2; hence, they are only allowed access to the events from Amazon EC2.

See the following table for a comparison of Policy A and Policy B:

Event Pattern	Allowed by Policy A	Allowed by Policy B
{ "source": ["aws.ec2"]}	Yes	Yes
{ "source": ["aws.ec2", "aws.s3"]}	Yes	No (Source aws.s3 is not allowed)
{ "source": ["aws.ec2"], "detail-type": ["EC2 Instance State-change Notification"]}	Yes	Yes

Event Pattern	Allowed by Policy A	Allowed by Policy B
{ "detail-type": ["EC2 Instance State-change Notification"]}	Yes	No (Source must be specified)

Example 2: Define Multiple Sources That Can Be Used in an Event Pattern Individually

The following policy allows events from Amazon EC2 or CloudWatch Events. In other words, it allows an IAM user or role to create a rule where the source in the EventPattern is specified as either "aws.ec2" or "aws.ecs". Not defining the source results in a "deny".

```
1  {
2      "Version": "2012-10-17",
3      "Statement": [
4          {
5              "Sid": "AllowPutRuleIfSourceIsEC2OrECS",
6              "Effect": "Allow",
7              "Action": "events:PutRule",
8              "Resource": "*",
9              "Condition": {
10                 "StringEquals": {
11                     "events:source": [ "aws.ec2", "aws.ecs" ]
12                 }
13             }
14         }
15     ]
16 }
```

See the following table for examples of event patterns that would be allowed or denied by this policy:

Event Pattern	Allowed by the Policy
{ "source": ["aws.ec2"]}	Yes
{ "source": ["aws.ecs"]}	Yes
{ "source": ["aws.s3"]}	No
{ "source": ["aws.ec2", "aws.ecs"]}	No
{ "detail-type": ["AWS API Call via CloudTrail"]}	No

Example 3: Define a Source and a DetailType That Can Be Used in an Event Pattern

The following policy allows events only from the `aws.ec2` source with DetailType equal to `EC2 instance state change notification`.

```
1  {
2      "Version": "2012-10-17",
3      "Statement": [
4          {
5              "Sid": "AllowPutRuleIfSourceIsEC2AndDetailTypeIsInstanceStateChangeNotification",
6              "Effect": "Allow",
```

```
 7          "Action": "events:PutRule",
 8          "Resource": "*",
 9          "Condition": {
10              "StringEquals": {
11                  "events:source": "aws.ec2",
12                  "events:detail-type": "EC2 Instance State-change Notification"
13              }
14          }
15      }
16  ]
17 }
```

See the following table for examples of event patterns that would be allowed or denied by this policy:

Event Pattern	Allowed by the Policy
{ "source": ["aws.ec2"]}	No
{ "source": ["aws.ecs"]}	No
{ "source": ["aws.ec2"], "detail-type": ["EC2 Instance State-change Notification"]}	Yes
{ "source": ["aws.ec2"], "detail-type": ["EC2 Instance Health Failed"]}	No
{ "detail-type": ["EC2 Instance State-change Notification"]}	No

Example 4: Ensure That the Source Is Defined in the Event Pattern

The following policy allows creating rules with `EventPatterns` that must have the source field. In other words, an IAM user or role can't create a rule with an `EventPattern` that does not provide a specific source.

```
 1 {
 2      "Version": "2012-10-17",
 3      "Statement": [
 4          {
 5              "Sid": "AllowPutRuleIfSourceIsSpecified",
 6              "Effect": "Allow",
 7              "Action": "events:PutRule",
 8              "Resource": "*",
 9              "Condition": {
10                  "Null": {
11                      "events:source": "false"
12                  }
13              }
14          }
15      ]
16 }
```

See the following table for examples of event patterns that would be allowed or denied by this policy:

Event Pattern	Allowed by the Policy
{ "source": ["aws.ec2"], "detail-type": ["EC2 Instance State-change Notification"]}	Yes
{ "source": ["aws.ecs", "aws.ec2"]}	Yes

126

Event Pattern	Allowed by the Policy
{ "detail-type": ["EC2 Instance State-change Notification"]}	No

Example 5: Define a List of Allowed Sources in an Event Pattern with Multiple Sources

The following policy allows creating rules with `EventPatterns` that can have multiple sources in them. Each source listed in the event pattern must be a member of the list provided in the condition. When using the ForAllValues condition, make sure that at least one of the items in the condition list is defined.

```
 1 {
 2     "Version": "2012-10-17",
 3     "Statement": [
 4         {
 5             "Sid": "AllowPutRuleIfSourceIsSpecifiedAndIsEitherS3OrEC2OrBoth",
 6             "Effect": "Allow",
 7             "Action": "events:PutRule",
 8             "Resource": "*",
 9             "Condition": {
10                 "ForAllValues:StringEquals": {
11                     "events:source": [ "aws.ec2", "aws.s3" ]
12                 },
13                 "Null": {
14                     "events:source": "false"
15                 }
16             }
17         }
18     ]
19 }
```

See the following table for examples of event patterns that would be allowed or denied by this policy:

Event Pattern	Allowed by the Policy
{ "source": ["aws.ec2"]}	Yes
{ "source": ["aws.ec2", "aws.s3"]}	Yes
{ "source": ["aws.ec2", "aws.autoscaling"]}	No
{ "detail-type": ["EC2 Instance State-change Notification"]}	No

Example 6: Ensure That AWS CloudTrail Events for API Calls from a Certain PrincipalId Are Consumed

All AWS CloudTrail events have the ID of the user who made the API call (PrincipalId) in the `detail.userIdentity.principalId` path of an event. With the help of the `events:detail.userIdentity.principalId` condition key, you can limit the access of IAM users or roles to the CloudTrail events for only those coming from a specific account.

```
 1     "Version": "2012-10-17",
 2     "Statement": [
 3         {
```

```
4              "Sid": "AllowPutRuleOnlyForCloudTrailEventsWhereUserIsASpecificIAMUser",
5              "Effect": "Allow",
6              "Action": "events:PutRule",
7              "Resource": "*",
8              "Condition": {
9                  "StringEquals": {
10                     "events:detail-type": [ "AWS API Call via CloudTrail" ],
11                     "events:detail.userIdentity.principalId": [ "AIDAJ45Q7YFFAREXAMPLE" ]
12                 }
13             }
14         }
15     ]
16 }
```

See the following table for examples of event patterns that would be allowed or denied by this policy:

Event Pattern	Allowed by the Policy
{ "detail-type": ["AWS API Call via Cloud-Trail"]}	No
{ "detail-type": ["AWS API Call via Cloud-Trail"], "detail.userIdentity.principalId": ["AIDAJ45Q7YFFAREXAMPLE"]}	Yes
{ "detail-type": ["AWS API Call via Cloud-Trail"], "detail.userIdentity.principalId": ["AROAIDPPEZS35WEXAMPLE:AssumedRoleSessionName"]}	No

Example 7: Limiting Access to Targets

If an IAM user or role has events:PutTargets permission, they can add any target under the same account to the rules that they are allowed to access. For example, the following policy limits adding targets to only a specific rule (MyRule under account 123456789012).

```
1 {
2     "Version": "2012-10-17",
3     "Statement": [
4         {
5             "Sid": "AllowPutTargetsOnASpecificRule",
6             "Effect": "Allow",
7             "Action": "events:PutTargets",
8             "Resource": "arn:aws:events:us-east-1:123456789012:rule/MyRule"
9         }
10     ]
11 }
```

To limit what target can be added to the rule, use the events:TargetArn condition key. For example, you can limit targets to only Lambda functions, as in the following example.

```
1 {
2     "Version": "2012-10-17",
3     "Statement": [
4         {
5             "Sid": "AllowPutTargetsOnASpecificRuleAndOnlyLambdaFunctions",
6             "Effect": "Allow",
```

```
 7          "Action": "events:PutTargets",
 8          "Resource": "arn:aws:events:us-east-1:123456789012:rule/MyRule",
 9          "Condition": {
10              "ArnLike": {
11                  "events:TargetArn": "arn:aws:lambda:*:*:function:*"
12              }
13          }
14      }
15    ]
16 }
```

Logging Amazon CloudWatch Events API Calls in AWS CloudTrail

AWS CloudTrail is a service that captures API calls made by or on behalf of your AWS account. This information is collected and written to log files that are stored in an Amazon S3 bucket that you specify. API calls are logged whenever you use the API, the console, or the AWS CLI. Using the information collected by CloudTrail, you can determine what request was made, the source IP address the request was made from, who made the request, when it was made, and so on.

To learn more about CloudTrail, including how to configure and enable it, see the What is AWS CloudTrail in the *AWS CloudTrail User Guide*.

Topics

- CloudWatch Events Information in CloudTrail
- Understanding Log File Entries

CloudWatch Events Information in CloudTrail

If CloudTrail logging is turned on, calls made to API actions are captured in log files. Every log file entry contains information about who generated the request. For example, if a request is made to create a CloudWatch Events rule (`PutRule`), CloudTrail logs the identity of the person or service that made the request.

The identity information in the log entry helps you determine the following:

- Whether the request was made with root or IAM user credentials
- Whether the request was made with temporary security credentials for a role or federated user
- Whether the request was made by another AWS service

For more information, see the CloudTrail userIdentity Element in the *AWS CloudTrail User Guide*.

You can store your log files in your bucket for as long as you want, but you can also define Amazon S3 lifecycle rules to archive or delete log files automatically. By default, your log files are encrypted by using Amazon S3 server-side encryption (SSE).

To be notified upon log file delivery, you can configure CloudTrail to publish Amazon SNS notifications when new log files are delivered. For more information, see Configuring Amazon SNS Notifications for CloudTrail in the *AWS CloudTrail User Guide*.

You can also aggregate Amazon CloudWatch Logs log files from multiple AWS regions and multiple AWS accounts into a single S3 bucket. For more information, see Receiving CloudTrail Log Files from Multiple Regions and Receiving CloudTrail Log Files from Multiple Accounts in the *AWS CloudTrail User Guide*.

When logging is turned on, the following API actions are written to CloudTrail:

- DeleteRule
- DescribeRule
- DisableRule
- EnableRule
- ListRuleNamesByTarget
- ListRules
- ListTargetsByRule
- PutRule
- PutTargets
- RemoveTargets
- TestEventPattern

For more information about these actions, see the Amazon CloudWatch Events API Reference.

Understanding Log File Entries

CloudTrail log files contain one or more log entries. Each entry lists multiple JSON-formatted events. A log entry represents a single request from any source and includes information about the requested action, the date and time of the action, request parameters, and so on. The log entries are not an ordered stack trace of the public API calls, so they do not appear in any specific order. Log file entries for all API actions are similar to the examples below.

The following log file entry shows that a user called the CloudWatch Events **PutRule** action.

```
1  {
2        "eventVersion":"1.03",
3        "userIdentity":{
4           "type":"Root",
5           "principalId":"123456789012",
6           "arn":"arn:aws:iam::123456789012:root",
7           "accountId":"123456789012",
8           "accessKeyId":"AKIAIOSFODNN7EXAMPLE",
9           "sessionContext":{
10             "attributes":{
11                "mfaAuthenticated":"false",
12                "creationDate":"2015-11-17T23:56:15Z"
13             }
14          }
15       },
16       "eventTime":"2015-11-18T00:11:28Z",
17       "eventSource":"events.amazonaws.com",
18       "eventName":"PutRule",
19       "awsRegion":"us-east-1",
20       "sourceIPAddress":"AWS Internal",
21       "userAgent":"AWS CloudWatch Console",
22       "requestParameters":{
23          "description":"",
24          "name":"cttest2",
25          "state":"ENABLED",
26          "eventPattern":"{\"source\":[\"aws.ec2\"],\"detail-type\":[\"EC2 Instance State-
               change Notification\"]}",
27          "scheduleExpression":""
28       },
29       "responseElements":{
30          "ruleArn":"arn:aws:events:us-east-1:123456789012:rule/cttest2"
31       },
32       "requestID":"e9caf887-8d88-11e5-a331-3332aa445952",
33       "eventID":"49d14f36-6450-44a5-a501-b0fdcdfaeb98",
34       "eventType":"AwsApiCall",
35       "apiVersion":"2015-10-07",
36       "recipientAccountId":"123456789012"
37  }
```

Troubleshooting CloudWatch Events

You can use the steps in this section to troubleshoot CloudWatch Events.

Topics

- My rule was triggered but my Lambda function was not invoked
- I have just created/modified a rule but it did not match a test event
- My rule did not self-trigger at the time specified in the ScheduleExpression
- My rule did not trigger at the time that I expected
- My rule matches IAM API calls but my rule was not triggered
- My rule is not working because the IAM role associated with the rule is ignored when the rule is triggered
- I created a rule with an EventPattern that is supposed to match a resource, but I don't see any events that match the rule
- My event's delivery to the target experienced a delay
- My rule was triggered more than once in response to two identical events. What guarantee does CloudWatch Events offer for triggering rules or delivering events to the targets?
- My events are not delivered to the target Amazon SQS queue
- My rule is being triggered but I don't see any messages published into my Amazon SNS topic
- My Amazon SNS topic still has permissions for CloudWatch Events even after I deleted the rule associated with the Amazon SNS topic
- Which IAM condition keys can I use with CloudWatch Events
- How can I tell when CloudWatch Events rules are broken

My rule was triggered but my Lambda function was not invoked

Make sure you have the right permissions set for your Lambda function. Run the following command using AWS CLI (replace the function name with your function and use the AWS Region your function is in):

```
1 aws lambda get-policy --function-name MyFunction --region us-east-1
```

You should see an output similar to the following:

```
1  {
2      "Policy": "{\"Version\":\"2012-10-17\",
3      \"Statement\":[
4          {\"Condition\":{\"ArnLike\":{\"AWS:SourceArn\":\"arn:aws:events:us-east-1:123456789012:
               rule/MyRule\"}},
5          \"Action\":\"lambda:InvokeFunction\",
6          \"Resource\":\"arn:aws:lambda:us-east-1:123456789012:function:MyFunction\",
7          \"Effect\":\"Allow\",
8          \"Principal\":{\"Service\":\"events.amazonaws.com\"},
9          \"Sid\":\"MyId\"}
10     ],
11     \"Id\":\"default\"}"
12 }
```

If you see the following:

```
1 A client error (ResourceNotFoundException) occurred when calling the GetPolicy operation: The
     resource you requested does not exist.
```

Or, you see the output but you can't locate events.amazonaws.com as a trusted entity in the policy, run the following command:

```
1 aws lambda add-permission \
2 --function-name MyFunction \
3 --statement-id MyId \
4 --action 'lambda:InvokeFunction' \
5 --principal events.amazonaws.com \
6 --source-arn arn:aws:events:us-east-1:123456789012:rule/MyRule
```

Note

If the policy is incorrect, you can also edit the rule in the CloudWatch Events console by removing and then adding it back to the rule. The CloudWatch Events console will set the correct permissions on the target.

If you're using a specific Lambda alias or version, you must add the `--qualifier` parameter in the `aws lambda get-policy` and `aws lambda add-permission` commands.

```
1 aws lambda add-permission \
2 --function-name MyFunction \
3 --statement-id MyId \
4 --action 'lambda:InvokeFunction' \
5 --principal events.amazonaws.com \
6 --source-arn arn:aws:events:us-east-1:123456789012:rule/MyRule
7 --qualifier alias or version
```

Another reason the Lambda function would fail to trigger is if the policy you see when running `get-policy` contains a `SourceAccount` field. A `SourceAccount` setting prevents CloudWatch Events from being able to invoke the function.

I have just created/modified a rule but it did not match a test event

When you make a change to a rule or to its targets, incoming events might not immediately start or stop matching to new or updated rules. Allow a short period of time for changes to take effect. If, after this short period, events still do not match, you can also check several Events metrics for your rule in CloudWatch such as `TriggeredRules`, `Invocations`, and `FailedInvocations` for further debugging.

You can also use the `TestEventPattern` action to test the event pattern of your rule with a test event to make sure the event pattern of your rule is correctly set. For more information, see TestEventPattern in the *Amazon CloudWatch Events API Reference*.

My rule did not self-trigger at the time specified in the ScheduleExpression

ScheduleExpressions are in UTC. Make sure you have set the schedule for rule to self-trigger in the UTC timezone. If the ScheduleExpression is correct, then follow the steps under I have just created/modified a rule but it did not match a test event.

My rule did not trigger at the time that I expected

CloudWatch Events doesn't support setting an exact start time when you create a rule to run every time period. The count down to run time begins as soon as you create the rule.

You can use a cron expression to invoke targets at a specified time. For example, you can use a cron expression to create a rule that is triggered every 4 hours exactly on 0 minute. In the CloudWatch console, you'd use the cron expression 0 0/4 * * ? *, and with the AWS CLI you'd use the cron expression `cron(0 0/4 * * ? *)`. For example, to create a rule named TestRule that is triggered every 4 hours using the AWS CLI, you would type the following at a command prompt:

```
1 aws events put-rule --name TestRule --schedule-expression 'cron(0 0/4 * * ? *)'
```

You can use the 0/5 * * ? * cron expression to trigger a rule every 5 minutes. For example:

```
1  aws events put-rule --name TestRule --schedule-expression 'cron(0/5 * * ? *)'
```

CloudWatch Events does not provide second-level precision in schedule expressions. The finest resolution using a cron expression is a minute. Due to the distributed nature of the CloudWatch Events and the target services, the delay between the time the scheduled rule is triggered and the time the target service honors the execution of the target resource might be several seconds. Your scheduled rule will be triggered within that minute but not on the precise 0th second.

My rule matches IAM API calls but my rule was not triggered

The IAM service is only available in the US East (N. Virginia) Region, so any AWS API call events from IAM are only available in that region. For more information, see CloudWatch Events Event Examples From Each Supported Service.

My rule is not working because the IAM role associated with the rule is ignored when the rule is triggered

IAM roles for rules are only used for relating events to Kinesis streams. For Lambda functions and Amazon SNS topics, you need to provide resource-based permissions.

Make sure your regional AWS STS endpoints are enabled. CloudWatch Events talks to the regional AWS STS endpoints when assuming the IAM role you provided. For more information, see Activating and Deactivating AWS STS in an AWS Region in the *IAM User Guide*.

I created a rule with an EventPattern that is supposed to match a resource, but I don't see any events that match the rule

Most services in AWS treat the colon (:) or forward slash (/) as the same character in Amazon Resource Names (ARNs). However, CloudWatch Events uses an exact match in event patterns and rules. Be sure to use the correct ARN characters when creating event patterns so that they match the ARN syntax in the event to match.

Moreover, not every event has the resources field populated (such as AWS API call events from CloudTrail).

My event's delivery to the target experienced a delay

CloudWatch Events tries to deliver an event to a target for up to 24 hours. The first attempt is made as soon as the event arrives in the event stream. However, if the target service is having problems or your account is being throttled, CloudWatch Events automatically reschedules another delivery in the future. If 24 hours has passed since the arrival of event, no more attempts are scheduled and the FailedInvocations metric is published in CloudWatch.

My rule was triggered more than once in response to two identical events. What guarantee does CloudWatch Events offer for triggering rules or delivering events to the targets?

CloudWatch Events guarantees triggering a rule at least once in response to an event or to a schedule. In rare cases, the same rule can be triggered more than once for a single event or scheduled time, or the same target can be invoked more than once for a given triggered rule.

My events are not delivered to the target Amazon SQS queue

The Amazon SQS queue may be encrypted. If you create a rule with an encrypted Amazon SQS queue as a target, you must have the following section included in your KMS key policy for the event to be successfully delivered to the encrypted queue.

```
1  {
2              "Sid": "Allow CWE to use the key",
3              "Effect": "Allow",
4              "Principal": {
5                      "Service": "events.amazonaws.com"
6              },
7              "Action": [
8                      "kms:Decrypt",
9                      "kms:GenerateDataKey"
10             ],
11             "Resource": "*"
12 }
```

My rule is being triggered but I don't see any messages published into my Amazon SNS topic

Make sure you have the right permission set for your Amazon SNS topic. Run the following command using AWS CLI (replace the topic ARN with your topic and use the AWS Region your topic is in):

```
1  aws sns get-topic-attributes --region us-east-1 --topic-arn "arn:aws:sns:us-east-1:123456789012:
     MyTopic"
```

You should see policy attributes similar to the following:

```
1  "{\"Version\":\"2012-10-17\",
2  \"Id\":\"__default_policy_ID\",
3  \"Statement\":[{\"Sid\":\"__default_statement_ID\",
4  \"Effect\":\"Allow\",
5  \"Principal\":{\"AWS\":\"*\"},
6  \"Action\":[\"SNS:Subscribe\",
7  \"SNS:ListSubscriptionsByTopic\",
8  \"SNS:DeleteTopic\",
9  \"SNS:GetTopicAttributes\",
10 \"SNS:Publish\",
11 \"SNS:RemovePermission\",
12 \"SNS:AddPermission\",
13 \"SNS:Receive\",
14 \"SNS:SetTopicAttributes\"],
15 \"Resource\":\"arn:aws:sns:us-east-1:123456789012:MyTopic\",
16 \"Condition\":{\"StringEquals\":{\"AWS:SourceOwner\":\"123456789012\"}}},{\"Sid\":\"
     Allow_Publish_Events\",
17 \"Effect\":\"Allow\",
18 \"Principal\":{\"Service\":\"events.amazonaws.com\"},
19 \"Action\":\"sns:Publish\",
20 \"Resource\":\"arn:aws:sns:us-east-1:123456789012:MyTopic\"}]}"
```

If you see a policy similar to the following, you have only the default policy set:

```
1  "{\"Version\":\"2008-10-17\",
```

```
 2 \"Id\":\"__default_policy_ID\",
 3 \"Statement\":[{\"Sid\":\"__default_statement_ID\",
 4 \"Effect\":\"Allow\",
 5 \"Principal\":{\"AWS\":\"*\"},
 6 \"Action\":[\"SNS:Subscribe\",
 7 \"SNS:ListSubscriptionsByTopic\",
 8 \"SNS:DeleteTopic\",
 9 \"SNS:GetTopicAttributes\",
10 \"SNS:Publish\",
11 \"SNS:RemovePermission\",
12 \"SNS:AddPermission\",
13 \"SNS:Receive\",
14 \"SNS:SetTopicAttributes\"],
15 \"Resource\":\"arn:aws:sns:us-east-1:123456789012:MyTopic\",
16 \"Condition\":{\"StringEquals\":{\"AWS:SourceOwner\":\"123456789012\"}}}]}"
```

If you don't see events.amazonaws.com with Publish permission in your policy, use the AWS CLI to set topic policy attribute.

Copy the current policy and add the following statement to the list of statements:

```
1 {\"Sid\":\"Allow_Publish_Events\",
2 \"Effect\":\"Allow\",\"Principal\":{\"Service\":\"events.amazonaws.com\"},
3 \"Action\":\"sns:Publish\",
4 \"Resource\":\"arn:aws:sns:us-east-1:123456789012:MyTopic\"}
```

The new policy should look like the one described earlier.

Set topic attributes with the AWS CLI:

```
1 aws sns set-topic-attributes --region us-east-1 --topic-arn "arn:aws:sns:us-east-1:123456789012:
   MyTopic" --attribute-name Policy --attribute-value NEW_POLICY_STRING
```

Note
If the policy is incorrect, you can also edit the rule in the CloudWatch Events console by removing and then adding it back to the rule. CloudWatch Events sets the correct permissions on the target.

My Amazon SNS topic still has permissions for CloudWatch Events even after I deleted the rule associated with the Amazon SNS topic

When you create a rule with Amazon SNS as the target, CloudWatch Events adds the permission to your Amazon SNS topic on your behalf. If you delete the rule shortly after you create it, CloudWatch Events might be unable to remove the permission from your Amazon SNS topic. If this happens, you can remove the permission from the topic using the aws sns set-topic-attributes command. For more information about resource-based permissions for sending events, see Using Resource-Based Policies for CloudWatch Events.

Which IAM condition keys can I use with CloudWatch Events

CloudWatch Events supports the AWS-wide condition keys (see Available Keys in the *IAM User Guide*), plus the following service-specific condition keys. For more information, see Using IAM Policy Conditions for Fine-Grained Access Control.

How can I tell when CloudWatch Events rules are broken

You can use the following alarm to notify you when your CloudWatch Events rules are broken.

To create an alarm to alert when rules are broken

1. Open the CloudWatch console at https://console.aws.amazon.com/cloudwatch/.

2. Choose **Create Alarm**. In the **CloudWatch Metrics by Category** pane, choose **Events Metrics**.

3. In the list of metrics, select **FailedInvocations**.

4. Above the graph, choose **Statistic, Sum**.

5. For **Period**, choose a value, for example **5 minutes**. Choose **Next**.

6. Under **Alarm Threshold**, for **Name**, type a unique name for the alarm, for example **myFailedRules**. For **Description**, type a description of the alarm, for example **Rules are not delivering events to targets**.

7. For **is**, choose **>=** and **1**. For **for**, enter **10**.

8. Under **Actions**, for **Whenever this alarm**, choose **State is ALARM**.

9. For **Send notification to**, select an existing Amazon SNS topic or create a new one. To create a new topic, choose **New list**. Type a name for the new Amazon SNS topic, for example: **myFailedRules**.

10. For **Email list**, type a comma-separated list of email addresses to be notified when the alarm changes to the **ALARM** state.

11. Choose **Create Alarm**.

Document History

The following table describes the important changes to the *Amazon CloudWatch Events User Guide*.

Change	Description	Release Date
AWS CodeBuild as a target	Added AWS CodeBuild as a target for event rules. For more information, see Tutorial: Schedule Automated Builds Using AWS CodeBuild.	13 December 2017
AWS Batch as a target	Added AWS Batch as a target for Event rules. For more information, see AWS Batch Events.	8 September 2017
AWS CodePipeline and AWS Glue events	Added support for events from AWS CodePipeline and AWS Glue. For more information, see AWS CodePipeline Events and AWS Glue Events.	8 September 2017
AWS CodeBuild and AWS CodeCommit events	Added support for events from AWS CodeBuild and AWS CodeCommit. For more information, see AWS CodeBuild Events.	3 August 2017
Additional targets supported	AWS CodePipeline and Amazon Inspector can be targets of events.	29 June 2017
Support for sending and receiving events between AWS accounts	An AWS account can send events to another AWS account. For more information, see Sending and Receiving Events Between AWS Accounts.	29 June 2017
Additional targets supported	You can now set two additional AWS services as targets for event actions: Amazon EC2 instances (via Run Command), and Step Functions state machines. For more information, see Getting Started with Amazon CloudWatch Events.	7 March 2017
Amazon EMR events	Added support for events for Amazon EMR. For more information, see Amazon EMR Events.	7 March 2017
AWS Health events	Added support for events for AWS Health. For more information, see AWS Health Events.	1 December 2016
Amazon Elastic Container Service events	Added support for events for Amazon ECS. For more information, see Amazon ECS Events.	21 November 2016

Change	Description	Release Date
AWS Trusted Advisor events	Added support for events for Trusted Advisor. For more information, see AWS Trusted Advisor Events.	18 November 2016
Amazon Elastic Block Store events	Added support for events for Amazon EBS. For more information, see Amazon EBS Events.	14 November 2016
AWS CodeDeploy events	Added support for events for AWS CodeDeploy. For more information, see AWS CodeDeploy Events.	9 September 2016
Scheduled events with 1 minute granularity	Added support for scheduled events with 1 minute granularity. For more information, see Cron Expressions and Rate Expressions.	19 April 2016
Amazon Simple Queue Service queues as targets	Added support for Amazon SQS queues as targets. For more information, see What is Amazon CloudWatch Events?.	30 March 2016
Auto Scaling events	Added support for events for Auto Scaling lifecycle hooks. For more information, see Auto Scaling Events.	24 February 2016
New service	Initial release of CloudWatch Events.	14 January 2016

AWS Glossary

For the latest AWS terminology, see the AWS Glossary in the *AWS General Reference*.

www.ingramcontent.com/pod-product-compliance
Lightning Source LLC
LaVergne TN
LVHW082039050326

832904LV00005B/239